GREAT BRAND STORIES

WIZARD!
HARRY POTTER'S BRAND MAGIC

STEPHEN BROWN

CYANBOOKS

Copyright © 2005 Stephen Brown

First published in Great Britain in 2005 by
Cyan Books, an imprint of

Cyan Communications Limited
4.3 The Ziggurat
60–66 Saffron Hill
London
EC1N 8QX
www.cyanbooks.com

The right of Stephen Brown to be identified
as the author of this work has been asserted
by him in accordance with the Copyright,
Designs and Patents Act 1988.

A CIP record for this book is available
from the British Library

ISBN 1-904879-30-6

Illustrations by Iain McIntosh

Printed and bound in Great Britain by
TJ International, Padstow, Cornwall

CONTENTS

Preface 4

1 The Introductory Story 6

2 The Stories Story 16

3 The Author Story 32

4 The Books Story 48

5 The Cinema Story 64

6 The Secrets Story 82

7 The Spin-offs Story 94

8 The Critics Story 112

9 The Consumers Story 132

10 The Brands Story 152

11 The Concluding Story 170

The Endnotes Story 180

PREFACE

Is Harry Potter a brand? Is it a particularly virulent strain of viral marketing? If Harry Potter is a brand, is branding now such an insidious virus that it affects every area of our lives, even children's literature? "Yes" might be the honest answer. Because the success of Harry Potter is, without a doubt, the result of brilliantly effective marketing.

Stephen Brown explores the inexorable rise of Harry Potter to his current status as a worldwide wizard of the commercial world: the keeper of the philosopher's stone that turns base materials into gold. Some of this rise is due to luck; much of it is about exceptional marketing intuition. No textbooks were followed, but, as if by magic, a global brand was created, a brand that achieves the holy grail of marketing: absolute adoration by its adherents.

Stephen Brown is a marketing academic. And a Harry Potter fan. The two are not mutually exclusive. There are many more surprises here: for example, this is a book that jolts you awake and keeps you buzzing with the sheer energy of its writing. How many business books have that effect?

Wizard! is a book that will appeal to Harry Potter fans and marketing professionals alike. You will discover much about Harry Potter and about branding. Like all great brands, Harry Potter is a mixture of simplicity and multi-layered complexity. Stephen Brown digs down, layer by layer, looking at the brand from every angle to record the way Harry Potter has entered the world's consciousness and earned his place in the pantheon of marketing immortals.

In the end, *Wizard!* is a brilliant analysis not just of Harry Potter but of modern branding and marketing – a paean to the power of brands. It's an attempt to reclaim marketing to the fold of fun, all the more compelling for rejecting traditional notions and conventional analysis. Marketing professionals should read *Wizard!* and enjoy being challenged. Read it for its insights, ideas and inspiration, and for the realization that the future of successful brands will be rooted in storytelling, creativity and wonder.

There is magic and mystery at the heart of branding. When Stephen Brown waves his wand of words, he does not merely reveal that truth, but celebrates it for the joy it brings to everyday life.

Hail Stephen Brown, brand magician!

John Simmons
Series editor, *Great brand stories*

1

The Introductory Story

Any fool can write a novel but it takes real genius to sell it.

J. G. Ballard

HARRY POTTER AND THE SWARM OF STORIES

Harry Potter is marketing incarnate. The Harry Potter story is relevant to every marketer, consumer researcher and wannabe brand wizard. From virtually nothing in 1997, the Harry Potter brand is now worth $4 billion, or thereabouts.[1] While this is peanut buttons compared to megabrands like Microsoft, Boeing, Nike or Ikea, it's better than a poke in the eye with a sharp broomstick.

Harry Potter, what's more, is a model of best marketing practice. The brand has been brilliantly marketed.[2] It is a copybook example of how to do it, a case study for our time. True, the methods employed by Harry's handlers run counter to conventional marketing wisdom – as we shall see – but they are no less effective for all that.

So successful, in fact, has this brand building been that there can't be a single person anywhere who hasn't heard of Harry Potter and the bestselling books that bear his name.[3] A scarred and orphaned schoolboy who is maltreated by his stepparents and bullied by his stepbrother, Harry Potter discovers on his eleventh birthday that he possesses magical powers and is whisked off to Hogwarts School of Witchcraft and Wizardry, where he studies the magical curriculum, learns that an enchanted world co-exists alongside the everyday world of non-magical Muggles, makes friends with fellow pupils Hermione Granger and Ron Weasley, spends many a happy hour playing Quidditch, a kind of airborne basketball, and, not least, battles against the evil Lord Voldemort, who killed his parents, tried and failed to kill

Harry too and is determined to take over the wizarding world by hook, crook, curse, hex and analogous iniquitous means.

The books are just the start of it, moreover. The movies, the merchandise, the memorabilia, the media coverage, the maledictions of the critics, the make-a-quick-buck books *about* the phenomenon – ahem – all add to the sheer marketing magic surrounding the Harry Potter brand. Harry's great brand story is made up of multiple magical storylines, each relating to a different aspect of Pottermania, each with its own plot, progression and pay-off, each intertwined with, influenced by and intruding on the others.

Harry Potter, in effect, is a hive of stories. Harry Potter is a narrative honeypot. Harry Potter is buzzing.

RIDDIKULUS!

Many readers, I realize, are sure to remain unmoved by the above declarative paragraphs. For some, Harry Potter's status as a brand is debatable, to say the least. For others, the Harry Potter brand is irrelevant to them and their fellow members of the Widget Manufacturers & Metal Bashers Association. For yet others, the sticking point is my insinuation that branding is – or should be – a branch of the Magic Circle, the domain of wand-wielders, spell-casters and tremulous tea-leaf readers.

With regard to Harry's standing as a brand, it is true that the term has traditionally been reserved for fast-moving consumer goods like Häagen Dazs and Hellman's Mayonnaise, rather than fast-moving fictional characters like

Harry Potter or Sherlock Holmes. Brands and branding, however, have latterly spread their wings, taken flight and alighted on just about every conceivable surface. Celebrities, charities, colleges, consultants, conglomerates, city centres, conurbations and entire countries are now regarded as brands and treated as such by their constituents. Branding may be less well developed in these domains than in more conventional marketing categories like clothes, cars, computers and cosmetics, but that doesn't mean that creative artists or cartoon characters are any less brandable than convenience foods or credit cards. Harry Potter is as much a brand as David Beckham, Black & Decker and Dolce & Gabbana.

The doubts of the widget contingent are less easily dispelled, if only because the beliefs of the muck 'n' brass brigade are more deeply entrenched than most. Harry Potter is kids' stuff, they say. It is a teenage fad, a passing fancy, a moment of marketplace madness akin to Beanie Babies, Teletubbies, pet rocks, Rubik's cubes, Cabbage Patch dolls and, for those with very long memories, hula hoops and Davy Crockett coonskin caps. Hence, it has nothing to teach the rest of us, those with serious marketing matters to attend to.

Widespread though they are, such old-fashioned smokestack attitudes conveniently overlook the fact that we live in a new-aged, silicon-chipped world. We live in what has variously been described as an entertainment economy, an attention economy, a catwalk economy and, inevitably, a new economy. We are living, as Leadbeater airily observes, on thin air.[4] It follows that far from being tangential to today's commercial concerns, Harry Potter is typical of the world that most of us work in, sell to and negotiate daily. It also follows, as this essay shall seek to show, that we can learn more about branding from Harry Potter or Hello Kitty or Hennes & Mauritz than we can from HP Baked Beans, Head & Shoulders shampoo or Arm & Hammer toothpaste.

HARRY POTTER SPELLS MARKETING

Although many might concede that the Harry Potter phenomenon says something about twenty-first-century society in general and the contemporary branding condition in particular, even the most open-minded marketers are likely to balk at my magical aspirations. Marketing's proper aim, they maintain, is to become ever more rigorous, ever more analytical, ever more "scientific." Our profession's hard-edged quest is to identify meaningful metrics that provide irrefutable proof of marketing's contribution to the bottom line. Having done so, marketers will finally shed their slippery image, win recognition as serious corporate players and be carried in triumph to boardroom nirvana.[5]

Carried on their shields, more like. The notion that we are brand engineers or scientists – much less brand genome-splicers – is nonsense. The merest glance across the brandscape reveals that marketing is inherently magical. Our brand bestiary of talking dogs, dancing cats, flying cows, jolly green giants, trick-cycling sheep, cereal-shilling leprechauns, beer-pitching frogs, coke-quaffing polar bears et cetera is testament to marketing's intrinsic magic. We routinely employ bedazzling advertising appeals or claim, like stricken British retailer Marks & Spencer, to sell Magic and Sparkle. Our price reductions are never less than fantastic, incredible, extraordinary, miraculous or superhuman. They have to be seen to be believed. Even marketing education is not averse to magic spells, alliterative incantations, mandala-like matrices and any number of pedagogic abracadabras. Thus we have 3Cs, 4Ps, five forces, seven Ss, nine Os and, hey presto, 30Rs.[6] David Blaine has nothing on us.

THE UNBEARABLE LIGHTNESS OF BRANDING

It seems to me that far from being hard-edged, quants-focused and metrics-minded, marketing is mantic at heart. Sleight of hand is our signature stratagem, mumbo-jumbo our materiel. We have much to learn from Hogwarts School of Witchcraft and Wizardry. We have much to learn from creative writers like Joanne Rowling and the artistic community full stop. In this regard, the magical essence of branding is cogently captured in Alex Shakar's *The Savage Girl*,[7] a novel set in a cutting-edge marketing research agency. Brand-name products, one of the protagonists proclaims, help consumers construct a wonderful magical world above the workaday mundane world, a world of enchantment, allure and wish fulfilment:

> Our world exists only to hold up this other world, this ideal world. It's the world of our dreams, our desires. It's elaborate, it's heavy, and we carry it around with us everywhere. But we don't mind. The more that's up here, the better. Because up here is where we keep

all that's best in us. The more that's up here, the richer our imagination becomes.... Products are the material we use to build our world above the world.

(The Savage Girl, p. 51)

Great brands transport consumers to this "world above the world." Great brands are extra-ordinary. They enchant. They bewitch. And, in order to develop our bewitching abilities, we must look to magicians, mythologists, dreamweavers and, above all, storytellers. The human race is run on stories. We are storytelling animals, *homo narratans.* "Our very definition as human beings," Peter Brooks points out, "is very much bound up with the stories we tell about our own lives and the world in which we live."[8]

The business world included. Management gurus and learned commentators have recently woken up to humankind's tale-telling imperative. Having exhausted one-word solutions (synergy, re-engineering, disintermediation) and having run the gamut of acronyms, metaphors and mnemonics (TQM, CSR, relationships, warfare, 4Ps, 3Cs, etc.), the consultancy–industrial complex has belatedly discovered the power of parables, anecdotes, yarns, myths and more.[9] Storytelling is the management method du jour. "Tell the tale, make the sale" is the order of the day. Or to put it another way: No tale, no sale.

The present book attempts to add to this tale-telling, story-selling frenzy. It contends that the greatest brand stories are in fact multi-stories, stories piled upon stories, *Arabian Nights–, Canterbury Tales–, Cloud Atlas–*style. In a world where corporate storytelling is increasingly commonplace, it's no longer enough to tell a single story coherently. It must be a majestic brand story, a magical brand story, a multi-faceted brand story. It must be a story similar to that written by lapsed marketing man Salman Rushdie.

In *Haroun and the Sea of Stories*, a sublime hybrid of *Alice in Wonderland* and *The Wizard of Oz*, the son of a washed-up storyteller seeks the cause of his father's faltering abilities.[10] He discovers that his dad is a former subscriber to Story Water, which is secretly piped from a magical world where stirring sagas and telling tales are constantly on tap. It is also a world where an evil, story-phobic wizard is trying to poison the wellsprings of narrative. With the aid of three doughty companions, however, Haroun outwits the evil wizard, foils his nefarious narracidal ambitions and arranges the reconnection of his father's carbonated story supply.

Harry Potter is unrelated to Haroun Khalifa, as far as we know, but his sparkling brand story is channelled from the same supernatural reservoir.

Open sesame...

2

The Stories Story

Art is a big pumped-up operatic version of real life; it's the lie that tells the truth better than the truth does.

Chuck Palahniuk

BRANDACADABRA

Great brand stories come in many different forms, including tragedy, comedy, epic and romance.[1] Harry Potter is something else again. Harry Potter is the stuff of fairy tales. The Harry Potter story combines Cinderella-like transformations, the golden goose of good fortune and a Rumpelstiltskinny ability to spin straw into gold. Harry Potter is the Sleeping Beauty of brands, brought to life by the kiss of a handsome prince called Marketing.

Marketing is the magic word here, because Harry Potter is above all else a marketing phenomenon. It is marketing that has turned a strictly limited edition into an international bestseller. It is marketing that has transformed a schoolyard cult into a worldwide smash. It is marketing that has plastered Potter's portrait on just about everything from posters and pyjamas to cuddly toys and Coca-Cola bottles. It is marketing that has made Harry Potter what he is.

Many Potterites, I grant you, are in denial about marketing's part in Harry's progress. Harry Potter, they proclaim, has been hijacked by Beelzebubian brand strategists, Mephistophelian marketers and their infernal ilk. An innocent, authentic, grass-roots phenomenon has been appropriated, commodified and systematically exploited by meretricious money-grubbers, spawn-of-the-devil spin doctors and similar henchpersons of multinational capital.

Yet the stories themselves tell a different story. They are as much *about* marketing as the outcome of marketing. The books embody the brand. So much so that on reading the Harry Potter books, one can't help but be struck by the sheer amount of marketing they contain. They are chock-a-block with brands. They repeatedly deal with marketplace matters. They feature characters who embody the archetypal essence of marketing (see text panel on pp. 24–5). They refer to almost every element of the marketing mix, as well as aspects of buyer behaviour, corporate strategy, marketing research and much, much more.

Early in book 4, for example, one character is preparing a market research report on cheap continental cauldrons, most of which fail to conform to UK safety standards and must therefore be denied access to the great British market. Another aspiring importer wonders whether there is a niche in the UK market for flying carpets, the people-carriers of the wizarding world, only to be brusquely informed that the British will never give up their broomsticks, thank you very much.

Advertising comes in the shape of huge hoardings akin to electronic scoreboards at football stadiums, with constantly changing sales pitches for broomsticks ("The Bluebottle: A Broom for All the Family"), soap powders ("Mrs Skower's All-Purpose Magical Mess-Remover: No Pain, No Stain!") and outfitters ("Gladrags Wizardwear – London, Paris, Hogsmeade").

Pricing figures prominently too, both precisely (the exact cost of goods, such as dragon's liver, in the magical currency of Galleons, Sickles and Knuts) and more generally (Madam Malkin's Robes for All Occasions advertises its annual sale in the *Daily Prophet*).

Logistics also get a look-in, principally in the form of Floo powder (a magical mixture that transports wizards Santa

Claus–style to chimneys of their choice), Portkeys (graspable objects such as old shoes and empty cola cans that ferry groups of holders very long distances), the owl postal service (colour-coded, naturally, by breed and destination: big barn owls cover the country, tiny scops owls deal with local deliveries) and the emblematic Hogwarts Express (an old-fashioned steam train that takes pupils to and from the school and famously departs from platform 9¾ at King's Cross station).

NPD is not forgotten either. The books are bunged full of brilliantly conceived brands and new product concepts. Magical mirrors don't just reflect, they remark on the viewer's appearance ("Tuck your shirt in, scruffy," "You're fighting a losing battle there, dearie"). Clocks do more than tell the time; their dials announce "You're late" and the hands indicate one's whereabouts ("at the office," "in mortal peril"). Snapshots are animated, since the photographed objects understandably refuse to stand still ("Well, you can't expect him to hang around all day"). Garden gnomes are more than mere lawn art, they are the real thing – irritating pests that have to be forcibly uprooted, kicking and screaming all the while. Cauldrons are self-stirring; kitchen knives chop of their own accord; socks scream when they get too smelly. Exploding snap is an ever-popular card game; revealers are like rubbers in reverse, exposing what was written and erased; gobstones, a playground pastime akin to marbles, squirt foul-smelling fluid at losing players; chess pieces have minds of their own and give guidance on appropriate moves. Hogwarts' list of banned objects includes Screaming Yo-Yos, Fanged Frisbees and Ever-Bashing Boomerangs.

Christmas crackers erupt like Vesuvius, showering the combatants with magical largesse: white mice, wizards' hats, non-explodable balloons, grow-your-own warts kits and more besides.

However, of all the product categories contained in the Harry Potter books, confectionery is the most fully realized. Rowling's remarkable array of sweets ranges from Cockroach Clusters, Jelly Slugs and Canary Creams to Chocolate Frogs, Sugar Quills (perfect for sucking surreptitiously in class) and her *pièce de resistance*, Bertie Bott's Every-Flavour Beans. As the brand name implies, these come in *every* conceivable flavour: chocolate, peppermint, marmalade, toast, coconut, baked bean, strawberry, curry, grass, coffee, sardine, sprouts, spinach, liver, tripe, earwax, nose-pickings and vomit. Aptly, their advertising slogan is "A Risk with Every Mouthful!"

MARKETING FOR MUGGLES

Brilliant though Bertie Bott's Beans are, it's important to appreciate that Rowling's brand concepts are more than mere scene-setting or infill. Marketing matters are central to the plots. Each book contains a major marketing-related set-piece that drives the story forward.

In the first volume, *Harry Potter and the Philosopher's Stone*, the commercial centrepiece is Diagon Alley, a magical shopping street that abuts London's Charing Cross Road.[2] It is accessed via an invisible public house between a record shop and a bookstore. When a secret brick in the Leaky Cauldron's back yard is depressed, the wall parts like the Red Sea to reveal a cobbled street lined with bewitched and bewitching retail establishments. Gringotts, an imposing goblin-guarded bank, dominates the scene and provides the all-important plot driver (the Philosopher's Stone is hidden in one of its safety-deposit chambers). However, the financial institution is just one among many striking premises along the twisting, turning thoroughfare. Here, a cauldron seller ("Cauldrons – All Sizes – Copper, Brass, Pewter, Silver – Self-Stirring – Collapsible"); there, an owl outlet ("Eeylops Owl Emporium – Tawny, Screech, Barn, Brown and Snowy"); and over there an exclusive broomstick dealership ("the new Nimbus Two Thousand – fastest ever").

The most important establishments, nevertheless, are Madam Malkin's Robes for All Occasions, where Harry is supplied with his official Hogwarts regalia and meets a poisonous fellow pupil, Draco Malfoy, for good measure; Flourish and Blotts bookstore, which stocks all the texts he'll be needing for his first year (*Magical Theory* by Adalbert Waffling, *Magical Drafts and Potions* by Arsenius Jigger, *The Dark Forces: A Guide to Self-Protection* by Quentin Trimble, among others); and, last but not least, an extremely long-established, deeply old-fashioned purveyor of fine wands, whose retail atmospherics are a cross between Savile Row bespoke tailoring and a 1950s-style haberdashers that has seen better days:

> The last shop was narrow and shabby. Peeling gold letters over the door read *Ollivanders: Makers of Fine Wands since 382 BC*. A single wand lay on a faded purple cushion in the dusty window.

> A tinkling bell rang somewhere in the depths of the shop as they stepped inside. It was a tiny place, empty except for a single spindly chair which Hagrid sat on to wait. . . . The very dust and silence in here seemed to tingle with some secret magic.
>
> (*Philosopher's Stone*, p. 63)

THINK GILDEROY, ACT LOCKHART

The second book, *Harry Potter and the Chamber of Secrets*, also features a fantastic marketing creation in the form of a publicity-seeking celebrity author who takes up a temporary teaching position at Hogwarts.[3] The epitome of self-marketing, Gilderoy Lockhart is a commercial grotesque, a latter-day P. T. Barnum, a twenty-first-century Wizard of Oz. Handsome, hirsute, expensively attired and orthodontically enhanced, Lockhart is five-times winner of *Witch Weekly's* Most-Charming-Smile Award and, *à la* Richard Branson, "It was remarkable how he could show every one of those brilliant teeth even when he wasn't talking." Like a book-writing Barry Manilow, he is adored by witches of a certain age; he bestrides the bestsellers list with his arresting adventures among outré occultists (*Gadding with Ghouls, Holidays with Hags, Travels with Trolls*, etc.); and he is a lion of the book-marketing circuit, where he draws huge crowds to his signings, readings and fan-club conventions. He even has a special quill made from an enormous peacock feather for such autograph-hungry occasions. Never let it be said, however, that all the attention has gone to Lockhart's head or that he has forgotten his roots. On the contrary, his secret

ROWLING'S MARKETYPES

Gilderoy Lockhart isn't the only marketing grotesque in Harry Potter. The entire spectrum of marketing stereotypes is portrayed:

Vernon Dursley, Harry's horrid stepfather, works in a sales capacity for Grunnings, an old-economy, metal-bashing manufacturing firm. When we meet him in the first book, he is anticipating a large order for drills. In the second, he wines and dines an important client, only to have his sales pitch ruined by the apprentice wizard upstairs. And in the third, sales have obviously picked up because he is rewarded with a new company car. Vernon is the antithesis of Gilderoy. He is a marketer in the nit-picking Kolterite tradition, obsessed with order, planning, precision, control. He disapproves of imagination. He is marketing science writ large. Very large.

Mundungus Fletcher is a ducker and diver, someone whose dealings are dodgy at best and illegal at worst. Mundungus is the Del Boy of the wizarding world, the kind of person who can supply batches of cauldrons that have fallen off the back of a broomstick or items that are unobtainable through legitimate channels of magical distribution (Knarl quills, venomous Tentacula seeds and similar Class C Non-Tradeable Substances). Just like Del, Mundungus recounts hilarious stories of his con-artistry, such as the

ambition is to "rid the world of evil and market my own range of hair-care potions."

For all his smarmy personal charm, Gilderoy Lockhart is a complete con artist. He is a disastrous teacher who possesses no meaningful magical skills, despite the self-serving stories in his vainglorious potboilers. When it comes to the crunch, what's more, he exhibits cowardice in the face of the enemy, the serpentine occupant of the Chamber of Secrets. Worse still, it is revealed that he doesn't actually write his own books, but steals the ideas from other, less photogenic wizards:

time he acquired a haul of hot toads and sold them back to their original owner, a "gormless gargoyle."

Dobby the house-elf is an unctuous Uriah Heep of a helpmeet, who does as he is bid, lives for the welfare of his paymasters and generally irritates all concerned, despite being a do-gooder at heart. If ever there were a perfect pen portrait of marketing's creepy, customer-coddling, pseudo-solicitous mindset, then it's embodied in Dobby. He's smarmy, he's obsequious, he's deeply unattractive, notwithstanding his sycophantic attempts at ingratiation. Dobby epitomizes what people really think of oily marketing types who proclaim that the customer is king, number 1, the be-all and end-all of business. Yeah, right.

Lord Voldemort is Harry Potter's arch-enemy, the acme of evil, the worst a man can get. He is marketing seen from the perspective of the anti-corporate, anti-capitalist, anti-globalization contingent. Marketing, they believe, is a monster that's bent on taking over the world: a monster that destroys everything it touches, a monster that sucks the blood of unicorns, a monster that's descended from the primal marketing person, the serpent in the Garden of Eden. It's entirely appropriate that the principal Harry Potter parodies, Michael Gerber's *Barry Trotter* books, depict Lord Voldemort as Lord Valumart, a marketing-minded megalomaniac.

'You mean you're *running away?*' said Harry disbelievingly. 'After all that stuff you did in your books?'

'Books can be misleading,' said Lockhart delicately.

(Chamber of Secrets, p. 220)

BLACK MAGIC

If Gilderoy Lockhart epitomizes the Barnumesque side of marketing, the shamelessly hyperbolic facet that finds contemporary expression in the likes of Michael O'Leary, Larry Ellison and Don King (see text panel), the third book engages with mainstream marketing matters. The plot of *Harry Potter and the Prisoner of Azkaban* is propelled by a brand-name broomstick, bought for the boy by the jailbird in question.[4] Granted, Harry Potter is ignorant of the source of the gift, to say nothing of his relationship to the mysterious gift-giver, an escaped mass murderer called Sirius Black. But what a present! What a product! What a brand! The BMW of broomsticks, the Ferrari of flying household effects, a veritable Porsche Carrera of aeronautically engineered cleaning appliances, the Firebolt is top of the top of the range. It not only carries the plot, it permeates the entire book.

As is often the case with the HP stories, the central marketing object makes an early appearance, in the show window of a Diagon Alley broomstick dealership. Fighting his way through an excited crowd of onlookers, Harry is stopped in his tracks by "the most magnificent broom he had ever seen in his life." So enraptured is our hero that he returns again and again to stare, agog, at the precious, perfect product, and when it turns up as an unexpected Christmas present, Harry and Ron sit transfixed, admiring the Firebolt from every angle, only to have it confiscated for fear that it is cursed. It is stripped down and carefully examined, to Harry's horror, but returned a few hours before an important inter-house Quidditch match. The rebuilt broomstick is carried in triumph through the school, attracting awestruck admiration wherever it goes ("Can I just hold it, Harry?"). Its aura encourages the sports mistress to wax lyrical about great racing brooms of the past ("reminds me of the old Silver Arrows"). And when the big game finally commences, the official announcer spends more time describing the Firebolt's attributes than commentating on the match ("Jordan! Are you being paid to advertise Firebolts? Get on with the commentary!") Potter's team triumphs, naturally enough, and it is eventually revealed that Sirius Black is neither a mass murderer nor trying to kill Harry Potter. On the contrary, he is Harry's godfather, who bought the Firebolt to make amends for fourteen years of missing Christmas presents.

WHIZ OF A WIZ

The fabulous Firebolt, furthermore, figures prominently in the fourth book, *Harry Potter and the Goblet of Fire.*[5] On this occasion, it is the Irish national team's broomstick brand of choice which they deploy in the book's opening marketing extravaganza, the Quidditch World Cup. Thanks to Mr Weasley's connections in the Ministry of Magic, Ron and Harry manage to get tickets for the final between Ireland and Bulgaria. And it is this that sets the plot in motion – or rather, certain mysterious occurrences in the immediate aftermath of the tournament. Before the narrative takes off, however, Rowling treats her readers to an entertaining description of the Quidditch Cup Final and the marketing razzamatazz that attends all such major sporting events. This includes the elaborate logistics necessary to transport 100,000 wizards to the invisible stadium without attracting the attention of non-magical Muggles; the totally over-the-top pre-game build-up by the respective national team cheerleaders (the Bulgarian mascots perform an erotic dance routine, Irish leprechauns shower the crowd with fake gold coins); and the egregious over-commercialization of the event, thanks to the profiteering activities of team sponsors, outdoor advertising agencies and ravening hordes of unofficial memorabilia vendors:

> Salesmen were Apparating every few feet, carrying trays and pushing carts full of extraordinary merchandise. There were luminous rosettes – green for Ireland, red for Bulgaria – which were squealing the names of the players, pointed green hats bedecked with dancing shamrocks, Bulgarian scarves adorned with lions that really roared, flags from both countries which played their national anthems as they were waved; there were tiny models of Firebolts, which really flew, and collectible figures of famous players, which strolled across the palm of your hand, preening themselves.
>
> *(Goblet of Fire*, p. 85)

PHOENIX KNIGHTS

The Quidditch World Cup, admittedly, is only a prelude to the Triwizard Tournament, which is won by Harry Potter despite stiff competition from the champions of Europe's top three wizardry schools and, inevitably, the malevolent endeavours of his nemesis, Lord Voldemort. Nemesis or not, He Who Must Not Be Named can't stop Harry collecting his Triwizard winnings, the princely sum of 1,000 Galleons. And it is this hard-won windfall that underwrites the action in book five, *Harry Potter and the Order of the Phoenix*.[6]

Revealing a hitherto unsuspected entrepreneurial bent, one that suggests a career in merchant banking may be beckoning, Harry invests in a magical joke shop operated by Ron Weasley's rambunctious brothers, Harry and George. Inveterate practical jokers who are determined to make serious money rather than follow in their father's time-serving footsteps, they spend much of the book developing, testing and retailing their product lines, which they sell house to house (and via owl mail order) while looking for permanent premises. Their range includes Extendable Ears, which enable people to eavesdrop on conversations in adjoining rooms; Bulbadox Powder, which brings the hapless dustee out in painful boils; Headless Hats, which render the wearer's head invisible, to the discombobulation of innocent bystanders; and Skiving Snackboxes, which contain a selection of snacks that make consumers sufficiently ill to avoid classwork for a few hours. This lip-smacking assortment ranges from Puking Pastilles and Fainting Fancies to Nosebleed Nougat and Fever Fudge (though the latter can inflict unfortunate side-effects on the taker's nether regions).

Never reluctant, moreover, to look a gift market in the mouth, Harry and George recruit gullible pupils to help perfect their product offer ("We regret that all work is undertaken at the applicant's own risk"); they treat Hogwarts as a massive marketing test-bed instead of an august educational institution ("We're going to use it to do a bit of market research, find out what the average Hogwarts student requires from a joke shop, carefully evaluate the results of our research, then produce products to fit the demand"); they sell their prototype Skiving Snackboxes to all and sundry (making 26 Galleons in a matter of minutes); and, before quitting the school for life in the boiler room of the enchanted-fireworks industry, they stage a spectacular product demonstration that does more to buzz their business than any number of small ads in the *Daily Prophet*.

The demonstration unfortunately consumes the entire stock of Weasleys' Wildfire Whiz-bangs. But its marketing effect is instantaneous, as orders flood in and waiting lists expand exponentially. So encouraging are the omens that, after staging one final PR stunt to mark the opening of their new emporium in Diagon Alley – a Portable Swamp, no less – the founders of Weasley's Wizarding Wheezes quit school, mount their broomsticks and speed off into the sunset. En route, no doubt, to the next marketing-saturated volume, *Harry Potter and the Half-Blood Prince*.[7]

Coming soon to a bookshop near you.

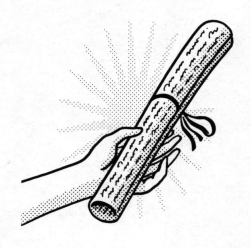

The Author Story

Literature nowadays is a trade. Putting aside men of genius, who may succeed by mere cosmic force, your successful man of letters is your successful tradesman. He thinks first and foremost of the markets; when one kind of goods begins to go off slackly, he is ready with something new and appetizing.

George Gissing

QUEEN MIDAS

King Midas, I'm sure you agree, has had a pretty bad press. Although his court was renowned for music, laughter, joy and ambrosial binge-drinking, Midas is remembered for two things only. First, he participated in ancient Greece's equivalent of *Pop Idol*, where he sat on the panel and made Simon Cowell-ish comments on the musical shortcomings of Apollo. So cloth-eared was the king that irate gods on nearby Olympus attached a pair of ass's ears to our unfortunate Attic jurist. Some say Simon should be similarly treated. Others say Cowell's ears are already up his ass. But not me, your honour.

Second, he encountered a wandering satyr called Silenus who was returning exhausted and hungry from the wars. A renowned storyteller, Silenus asked for Midas's assistance. The story-loving king agreed. As he recuperated, Silenus regaled the court with fantastic tales of Hyperborea, a cornucopian land where wine flowed like water and want was unknown. On his departure, the sated satyr granted the kindly king a wish, the world-famous wish that Midas soon wished he hadn't wished for. Gold on gold on gold, with gold trim and accessories, is a bit too Donald Trump for most people's taste. It's not so much a design statement as a yell from hell.

J. K. Rowling may not be yelling from hell, but she certainly knows the price of fame. Sure, the Harry Potter books and tie-ins have brought her untold wealth. Her personal fortune is estimated at £500 million. She is 96th on the *Sunday Times* 2005 Rich List, 84 places higher than Her Majesty the Queen.

She is sixth on *Forbes'* roll-call of female business leaders, and fifth on *Entertainment Weekly's* inventory of movers and shakers in the cultural industries. Although far from extravagant, she possesses palatial homes in Edinburgh (Merchiston), London (Kensington) and Perthshire (Killiechassie), and lives under a constant shower of leprechaun gold. Unlike the downpour at the Quidditch World Cup, though, Rowling's leprechaun gold is for real. They say she'll be a billionaire by the time Harry hangs up his Firebolt.[1]

In addition to the gold in them thar royalties, Rowling is liberally sprinkled with the glister of adulation. She has become something of a British national treasure. Her every gilded move or unguarded remark makes front-page headlines. Her books are regularly ranked among the country's all-time favourites. She is swaddled in literary awards (see list) and garlanded with honorary degrees from ancient seats of learning. She received an OBE in June 2000 for services to children's literature. She has been praised by Prince Charles, included in *Who's Who*, deemed worthy of abandonment on *Desert Island Discs* and lauded by lots of leading luvvies, including Stephen Fry, Richard Curtis, Griff Rhys Jones and the luvvy's luvvy himself, Sir Richard Attenborough.

Rowling's readings, what's more, are the literary equivalent of stadium rock. Not only has she filled London's Royal Albert Hall and Toronto's Skydome, but her gig in Vancouver attracted ticket touts and bootleg memento merchants. She's even copped a Grammy.[2] Can the call of the Hall of Fame be far away?

THE ADORATION OF THE MAGAZINES

Despite the fawning and fan worship, not to mention the dubious honour of coming runner-up to Dubya as *Time's* "Person of the Year 2000," there's a downside to this incessant adoration. As King Midas discovered to his cost, the golden touch is a mixed blessing at best and more trouble than it's worth at worst. Rowling may live in super-rich splendour, but fame and fortune have come at a heavy cost for this intensely private person. Her past life has been picked over by the tabloid press and what little dirty linen she possesses has been washed, scrubbed and hung out to dry in public. Her directionless pre-Potter existence, unfortunate family history, failed marriage to a Portuguese journalist and occasional economies with the truth, such as her claim to be born in salubrious Chipping Sodbury rather than insalubrious Yate, have been splashed across the redtops, to Rowling's understandable dismay.

Above and beyond the glittering goldfish bowl, which remains all too transparent, Joanne Rowling has been pestered by midlife-stricken stalkers, nagged by angry neighbours who object to the unsightly fortifications around her Merchiston mansion, and mocked for marrying a man who looks a wee bit like Harry Potter. Her every evening out, be it to a cinema, bar or restaurant, is reported in the gossip columns, thereby making return visits impossible on account of the crowds of well-wishers, rubber-neckers and autograph hunters. She has been accused, in classic tall-poppy fashion, of getting too big for her designer-label boots, refusing to listen to blue-pencil–brandishing apparatchiks and suffering the usual assortment of literary ailments including writers' block, nervous breakdown and authorial egomania. It is little wonder that Rowling reported in a BBC interview that she'd happily repay some of her fortune for the return of a private life.[3]

JKR AND THE BRANDSTALK

Of all the excess baggage that Harry the brand has brought with him, the item that weighs most heavily on Joanne Rowling is marketization. It is the relentless commodification of her creation that she finds especially unsettling. She has no time for fatuous publicity stunts. She is hesitant to shill the series on talk shows and webcasts. She has vowed that Harry Potter's image will never appear on Happy Meal containers, much less have an appetizing entrée named after him. She openly acknowledges her loathing for tie-in merchandise and is quite prepared to nix spinoffs that are too noisome for words (when a Moaning Myrtle toilet seat came up for discussion, she promptly put her foot down).

Yet, for all her anti-marketing attitude, the books belie Rowling's Big Bad Brand beliefs. If the stories tell us anything at all, aside from the obvious fact that her literary gifts are beyond compare, it is that JKR is a marketer manqué. Her ability to concoct compelling brand names, for example, is on a par with the best in our business: Jelly Slugs, Chocolate Frogs, Ogden's Old Firewhisky, Sleekeazy Hair Potion, Dr Ubbly's Oblivious Unction and so on. Compared to some of the horrors that marketing makeover artists have foisted on innocent products and organizations – Corus, Capita, Centrica, Carillion, Consignia, et cetera – Rowling's brand-naming acumen is as good as any and better than most. Is Citroën Xsara in the same league as Cleansweep Seven? Does Pfizer's Bextra stand up beside Barrufio's Brain Elixir? Ask yourself, is Giorgio Armani really a patch on Gladrags Wizardwear? Well, OK, I'll give you that one.

Rowling, what's more, has a wonderful ear for the rhetoric of sales brochures, recruitment posters and advice leaflets, as well as the absurdities of small-ad–speak. The careers literature in Hogwarts, to mention one among many, invariably commences with the overblown rhetorical questions that characterize the genre ("So You Think You'd Like to Work in Muggle Relations?," "Have You Got What it Takes to Train Security Trolls?") Kwikspell, likewise, is a pitch-perfect parody of a promotional flyer for self-improvement products:

> *Feel out of step in the world of modern magic? Find yourself making excuses not to perform simple spells? Ever been taunted for your woeful wandwork?*
>
> There is an answer!
>
> *Kwikspell is an all-new, fail-safe, quick-result, easy-learn course. Hundreds of witches and wizards have benefited from the Kwikspell method!*
>
> (Chamber of Secrets, pp. 97–8)

JK's greatest gift is reserved for senses of place and evocations of locations. Her descriptions of retail stores, shopping environments and trading places generally are right up there with the incomparable copywritings of Howard Gossage, David Ogilvy and Bruce Barton. Her portrayals of Hogwarts, or Diagon Alley, or Honeydukes sweetshop far surpass anything found in most official guidebooks or tourist brochures. They virtually compel the reader to hail a passing broomstick and get there before closing time, Gringotts' gold card akimbo:

> There were shelves upon shelves of the most succulent-looking sweets imaginable. Creamy chunks of nougat, shimmering pink squares of coconut ice, fat, honey-colored toffees; hundreds of different kinds of chocolate in neat rows; there was a large barrel of Every Flavour Beans, and another of Fizzing Whizzbees . . .
>
> *(Prisoner of Azkaban, p. 147)*

LITERARY INTERLUDE

There is, I confess, a slight problem with this line of argument. Literary types repeatedly tell us that we shouldn't confuse the "real" author with what appears in the books. It is unfair therefore to infer that Rowling is a marketer in disguise. Doing so is the scribbling equivalent of mistaking soap-opera characters for living, breathing people, or expecting stand-up comedians to be amusing in real life, or imagining that supermodels look the way they do in upmarket magazines. The Harry Potter books are fantasies, after all.

While it is easy to mistake the persona for the person, it is also true to say that most novelists, especially first-time novelists, freely draw on their personal experiences. They are encouraged to do so during creative writing courses and by the less-than-bestselling authors of those "How to Write a Bestseller" handbooks.

Rowling is no exception. Not unlike Tolkien, whose Great War experiences informed *Lord of the Rings*, Rowling's telling tales are intensely autobiographical.[4] Many of her characters are based on real people, and many of her most powerful passages are drawn from painful events in her past. Professor

Snape is a character sketch of John Nettleship, a stern chemistry teacher in Jo's old school, Wyedean Comprehensive. Ron Weasley is not only predicated on Séan Harris, Joanne's "foulweather friend," but Séan's blue Ford Anglia features in *The Chamber of Secrets*. The abominable Aunt Marge draws upon Rowling's incorrigible Aunt Frieda; Gilderoy Lockhart, it is rumoured, is a pen portrait of her first husband, Jorge Arantos; and the unspeakable Rita Skeeter is a composite of all the dirt-digging, rumour-spreading, quote-concocting, fact-inventing newspaper reporters who've poked their unwelcome noses into Rowling's private life.

What's more, the Dementors, ghoulish prison guards who suck the soul out of Azkaban's inmates, are a striking expression of Rowling's struggle with clinical depression. The Society for the Protection of Elvish Welfare (SPEW) is a homage to her time in Amnesty International. The emotional impact of her mother's untimely death – from multiple sclerosis, aged only 45 – is poignantly evoked in the first volume, when Harry looks in the Mirror of Erised (desire) and sees his long-dead parents for the first time.

A representation of Rowling's studious teenage self also appears in the books, though it is noteworthy that the name she chose, Hermione, is a female derivative of Hermes, the Greek god of the marketplace.[5] Rowling, remember, sets great store by the names of her characters. Just as Draco Malfoy, Remus Lupin, Argus Filch, Sirius Black, Dolores Umbridge, Minerva McGonagall et al. are indicative of the individual, so too Hermione says a lot about the author of the Harry Potter books.

BABBLING BRANDS

The texts, then, are unusually transparent, and inevitably Harryheads spend many a happy hour ruminating on the sources of, inspiration for and titbits hidden in Rowling's writings. Marketing titbits included. However, one doesn't need to scour the stories in order to get some sense of JK's commercial nous. It's readily apparent in real life as well. Indeed, for someone who is singularly protective of her literary creation, she has often acceded to marketing-enforced alterations. In the United States, the title of the first book was changed from *Philosopher's Stone* to *Sorcerer's Stone* in order to make it acceptable to the American market. The books were "translated" into American English to avoid any consumer confusion, and despite Rowling's contentions to the contrary, the US adjustments are fairly substantial.[6] Her very name was massaged to avoid deterring potential purchasers, on the erroneous assumption that teenage boys wouldn't buy books written by a woman. Whereas JK's OK, Joanne's a no-no.

Long before Joanne became JK, moreover, Rowling was getting in touch with her inner marketer. She worked for Manchester Chamber of Commerce; taught EFL to businessmen in Portugal; wrote two make-a-buck "adult" novels, which remain unpublished thus far; developed diverse novelty products, most notably card games, to educate her teenage charges in Leith Academy; and, while I hesitate to plunge into the psychological abyss, it is arguable that playing shop as a child in her grandfather's grocery store – after-hours, with real merchandise, just Jo and her younger sister, Di, in an empty supermarket – was a formative experience that helped shape her subsequent development. Unlike many no-logo ululating literati, JKR is a firm believer in the healing power of retail therapy (and has the rocks to prove it); she's quite content to write in commercial settings like pubs, restaurants and hotels (or she was before losing her anonymity); and, lest we forget, she market-researched the Harry Potter concept before completing the initial instalment. True, this market research simply involved asking her sister to read the first three chapters. However, Rowling acknowledges that had this surrogate customer not laughed, she'd have abandoned the whole Potter project.

Perhaps the most striking instance of the author's innate marketing acumen is the biographical story she's best known for. One of the series' perennial selling points, the early books in particular, is the legend of the single parent on public assistance who escapes her freezing unfurnished flat and pens the first book in Nicholson's café while her daughter snoozes in a stroller. Of late, Rowling has downplayed the details of this much-recycled myth (hey, the flat was heated!). She stresses her happy childhood, normal upbringing and successful if somewhat wayward post-college career before publishing the first barnstorming blockbuster. It was the dole-jockey legend, nevertheless, that attracted attention and generated press coverage. It was a pre-packaged PR fairytale that Rowling was quite prepared to go along with, to the extent of posing for photographs and being interviewed by reporters in Nicholson's. It was a primal rags-to-riches narrative that echoed the "poor boy makes good" arc of the Harry Potter saga itself and made her achievement all the more magical for consumers, booksellers, foreign publishers and the fourth estate's finest. If there is such a thing as journalistic catnip, then the tantalizing story of Edinburgh's coffee-shop Cinderella is the caviar of catnips.

To be sure, the Cinderella story is true and Rowling can hardly be held responsible for its ceaseless repetition. She could have refused to go along with the PR rigmarole, furthermore, but what first-time author is going to overrule her publisher's publicists? It could therefore be argued that Rowling is the victim of creative marketing storytelling rather than the ringleader. This may be so, but I doubt it. As we shall see, teasing, tantalizing and tormenting the customer is central to the Potter marketing strategy, and when it comes to teasing consumers, Rowling is a natural. She has a similar hold over the press, insofar as her much-publicized disdain for publicity acts like a red rag to the bulldozers of Fleet Street. As J. D. Salinger, Thomas Pynchon and Don DeLillo demonstrate, there's nothing more newsworthy than a newswary celebrity.

It doesn't end with teasing. Rowling is a natural in another sense. She is aware of her corporate social responsibilities. She gives generously to charities including Comic Relief and the Multiple Sclerosis Society, works tirelessly on behalf of the National Council for One Parent Families, and has spoken out on controversial issues such as student grants, welfare reform and the maltreatment of disabled children in Eastern Europe.

Unlike many apostles for CSR, JKR really means it. She remembers what it's like to have nothing. She lives to give. In truth, she has given something even greater than money or time. She has given book-reading a much-needed boost among Xbox-intoxicated teenage boys in particular, which is no mean achievement. If that's not CSR, I don't know what is.

RATTLES FROM THE SWILL BUCKET

The question nevertheless remains: why does Rowling downplay her marketing prowess and deny her remarkable brand-building acumen? Simple: it is an unavoidable career move in the scribbling business. Writers who want to be taken seriously can't confess to marketplace-mindedness, since it implies that they are grubby hacks who crank it out to order and have not only sold their souls to Mammon but are in cahoots with Mammon's marketing department. The horror, the horror...

This stance, incidentally, is particularly prevalent among writers whose books sell in large quantities or enjoy popular acclaim. Their less successful peers already regard them as literary Mudblooods and routinely accuse them of collusion with multinational capital. It would be a brave author indeed who admitted they were in it to earn a crust, let alone make obscene amounts of money.[7] Just as CEOs cannot admit to being anything other than 100 percent customer orientated, obsessed, focused, committed or whatever – even when their organizations are anything but – so too literary types must affect disdain for spin, hype, buzz, puff, plug, flog, sale and similar four-letter words. Until such time as Richard and Judy get in touch. Oprah even better.

The above, I grant you, is a gross caricature. The gulf between culture and commerce is getting narrower and narrower, as many studies have shown. The prevailing literary outlook, nonetheless, is still closer to George Orwell (who famously described advertising as the rattling of a stick in a swill bucket) than George Gissing (whose words of marketing wisdom serve as this chapter's epigraph). It follows that regardless of her real feelings about the Harry Potter hoopla, Joanne Rowling could never openly admit to being brand conscious, much less marketing literate. The fact that many highly regarded writers from Fay Weldon and F. Scott Fitzgerald to Elmore Leonard and Dorothy L. Sayers commenced their careers as swill-bucket rattlers is neither here nor there. Contemporary literary credibility demands disinterest in, detachment from and denial of what selling books actually involves. Selling.

Before we get all holier than thou, however, it must be noted that marketing is not immune to anti-marketing. In our hyper-hyperactive world of increasing advertising clutter, ever-expanding choice, product-range proliferation, brand names stretched beyond their elastic limit and wall-to-wall customer-centricity, one of the best ways of standing out from the clamouring crowd is by eschewing marketing completely. Sometimes the most effective form of marketing is not-marketing, non-marketing, un-marketing, call it what you will.

This is especially so when consumers are both marketing-savvy and marketing-sceptic, as many are at present, and in sectors such as fast-moving consumer goods where marketing has been around for longest and where every idea, approach and treatment has been tried several times over. Hence the latter-day advent of anti-brands, anti-ads, anti-products and anti-marketing marketing. Starbucks, The Body Shop, Ben & Jerry's, Innocent Drinks, Diesel jeans, Adbusters, Snapple, Sprite ("Image is nothing"), Levi's ("anti-fit jeans"), Yorkie ("Not for girls") and many more besides all sell on the basis of not selling.[8] As often as not, they are led by convincingly counter-cultural, conspicuously anti-corporate CEOs who express their contempt for materialism, overconsumption and the very capitalist system they are entangled in.

The Harry Potter phenomenon, in sum, is a literary analogue of The Body Shop or Starbucks. J. K. Rowling is the Anita Roddick of letters, the Howard Schultz of Hogsmeade.

Make mine a Hogwarts Expresso.

4

The Books Story

I wouldn't be surprised if today was known as Harry Potter Day in future – there will be books written about Harry – every child in our world will know his name!

Minerva McGonagall

THE PUBLISHER ON THE PEA

In 1835, a penniless author from the west of Denmark, the only son of a cobbler and a washerwoman, published a poorly printed pamphlet called *Eventyr, fortalte for Børn*.[1] It contained four "tales told for children," one of which recounted the story of a bedraggled young woman who appeared at the gate of a royal palace looking for shelter and claiming to be a princess. She was promptly put to the test – that old royal standby of a pea placed under twenty layers of sumptuous bedding – and next morning, wouldn't you know, she complained about her uncomfortable night. There was something hard in the bed. She was black and blue. She didn't get a wink. She had unwittingly passed the test. She was a real princess after all. More to the point, perhaps, she started the ball rolling for Hans Christian Andersen, who went on to fame, fortune and a permanent place in the fairy-story firmament.

One hundred and sixty-one years later, an impoverished single parent from the west of England, the eldest daughter of an aircraft engineer and a laboratory technician, submitted a self-typed manuscript to a literary agent in London. Unfortunately, Christopher Little didn't handle children's books, and *Harry Potter* was consigned to the tottering slush pile.[2] There it languished, like a forlorn legume under dozens of duvets, waiting for the chop at the hands of Bryony Evens, who was responsible for issuing the agency's unending stream of rejection letters. At a loose end one lunchtime, Bryony fished out the MS – luckily, it came encased in a distinctive black plastic wallet – and started reading. Captivated, she asked an agency reader, Fleur Howle, for a second opinion. Fleur too fell under Harry Potter's spell. Together our putative product champions persuaded Christopher Little to cast his expert eye over the boy wizard. Christopher succumbed, signed Rowling up and spread the news about his hotter than hot property. The rest is history.

Except that it isn't. The Harry Potter manuscript was spurned by twelve of London's leading publishing houses, including Penguin, Transworld and HarperCollins. A year or so later, the literary foundling landed on the doorstep of Bloomsbury, a small but perfectly formed publisher best known for Booker Prize–fighting fiction rather than kid lit. Fortunately, the newly appointed supremo of the children's division, former marketer Barry Cunningham, took a punt on the unwanted Potter property in the hope that it would raise the profile of his side of the house. He snapped up the penurious single parent, doled out a decidedly modest advance of £1,500 and, after meeting Rowling for lunch, disbursed some deathless words of wisdom to the first-time author: "You'll never make any money out of children's books, Jo."

ALL YOU NEED IS LOVEGOOD

Compared to some marketing mistakes, such as the New Coke calamity, the Firestone Tires imbroglio and Decca Records' infamous refusal to sign The Beatles, Cunningham's less than clairvoyant comments are of little or no consequence.[3] At least he had the gumption to get Rowling's signature, which is more than can be said for his less perspicacious peers at Penguin et al. As "rue the day" marketing decisions go, their collective rejection of Christopher Little's offer is way beyond hair-tearing, teeth-gnashing and cursing the literary Fates. It's on a par with the German schoolteacher who told ten-year-old Albert Einstein that he'd never amount to anything; the aeronautical engineer who maintained that manned flight by heavier-than-air machines was impossible, just three months before Wilbur and Orville took wing; and the good General Sedgwick's famous last words at the Battle of Spotsylvania in 1864, "They couldn't hit an elephant at this dist...."

And, boy, do Penguin and co. have good reason to regret the fact that Jo Rowling slipped through their fingers. To date, the first five books in her seven-book series have sold an estimated 250 million copies worldwide. They have been translated into 61 different languages, including Icelandic, Serbo-Croat, Vietnamese, Hebrew, Swahili, Ukrainian and Afrikaans, and are bestsellers in 200 countries and counting. According to the "Potter pottiness" index assembled by the *Guardian*, Australia, Germany, Japan and China are most entranced by the teenage wizard's adventures, though Mexico, Indonesia and India are not far behind.[4]

Nevertheless, the epicentres of the Potterquake remain the United Kingdom and, even more so, the United States of America, which accounts for approximately 55 percent of total sales. Harry Potter titles occupied the first four places on the *New York Times* bestseller list at one stage during their 98-week "run." Not since The Beatles' invasion of the mid-

1960s has the US surrendered so abjectly to a foreign cultural body, Ricky Martin included.

In Britain, meanwhile, the Potter titles have outsold everything under the sun, be it Bridget Jones or David Beckham, often by a factor of six or seven. Not only do they top every self-respecting bestseller list year in year out, but commentators are struggling to contextualize the sheer scale of Potter's triumph and to identify historical antecedents for such astonishing bibliohysteria. The best they can come up with is the 1812 publication of Lord Byron's *Childe Harold*, which brought central London traffic to a standstill, and the serialization of Charles Dickens' *The Old Curiosity Shop*, when massive crowds gathered to await the appearance of each and every arresting episode.

Mind you, if Harry Potter cops it in the final volume – as Rowling's love of Sydney Carton's noble exit in *A Tale of Two Cities* suggests he might – the ensuing national mourning will make the demise of Dickens' Little Nell look like New Year's Eve in Arcadia. During happy hour.

ACRONYMS ANYONE?

Above and beyond total sales figures, Harry's transatlantic hegemony is evident in every imaginable literary delivery vehicle. The books have been brought out in numerous forms – audio, Braille, large-type, illustrated, cloth-bound, download, box set – each of which has set the sub-category alight. No fewer than eighty variants of the US and UK editions are available, ranging from deluxe leather-bound gilt-trimmed gift sets (for American collectors with more dollars than sense) to dark and dowdy adult-covered versions (for Brits who don't want to be seen reading children's literature on the train). Novelty editions in Ancient Greek, Latin, Welsh and Gaelic have also been issued, as has a special set to commemorate 100 million sales worldwide. It is entirely appropriate, is it not, that a staggering marketing phenomenon should mark its staggering marketing achievements?

For many cynics, churls and sour-grapes–suckers, of course, Harry Potter is an egregious marketing concoction from start to finish. The success of the series is entirely due to hype, puff, hoopla and what have you. Faced with such accusations, the marketer's natural reaction isn't to deny our industry's desire-inducing abilities (since admitting that marketing has insignificant impact on consumer behaviour wouldn't go down well with corporate clients). Our unstated response, rather, is to wish it were so. If only it were true that marketing had the ability to command consumers' compliance and make them do as they're bid. The evidence, regrettably, suggests otherwise. Apart from the consistently calamitous failure rate of new product launches – received wisdom is that eight out of ten tank – the sad reality is that the *most* extravagantly hyped offers frequently fail at the point of sale. This is especially so in the cultural industries, where the grisly spectre of *Godzilla* still stalks the movie collectibles business and Robbie Williams' expensive attempt to crack the US market continues to amuse the music industry. The ego didn't so much land on Planet America as do a *Beagle 2* in Times Square.

Be that as it may, it is undeniable that the Harry Potter books have benefited from the ministrations of the caring commercial professions. The boy wizard's astonishing publishing achievements are predicated, at least in part, on time-grooved principles of book marketing. These principles, as is so often the case with brand building, are encapsulated in an ancient enchanted acronym that is protected by all sorts of hexes, hellhounds and secret bookbiz handshakes. The Chamber of Publishers' Secrets, however, has been penetrated on your behalf and I can hereby reveal that the acronym in question is ACCIO.

Modern book marketing involves five key elements – Author, Cover, Content, Interest and Obtainability – each one of which has been expertly deployed by Harry Potter's people:

Author. As Colin Bateman reveals in his scurrilous spoof *Chapter and Verse*, successful bookselling is increasingly reliant on authors who not only can tell a story well but *are* stories in and of themselves.[5] Pulchritude, disability, notoriety, celebrity and criminality – ideally all five – are as necessary nowadays as pellucid prose, striking metaphors and heart-stopping climaxes.

Within this general context, Joanne Rowling is manna from marketplace heaven, since her pre-fame personal circumstances are, if not quite Dickensian, certainly the stuff of Horatio Alger. Her post-fame struggles with the succubus of success are equally compelling, as are her extracurricular contributions to NGOs, educational institutions and good causes generally. Like Britney, Madonna, Damien Hirst and David Beckham, there's always something newsworthy about J. K. Rowling.

Cover. People may not judge books by their covers, but they definitely buy them by them. Eye-catching artwork can do wonders for sales, as the Taschen and Thames & Hudson imprints attest, though there's much more to covers than artwork. The title, typography, back-cover blurb and, not least, those priceless front-cover words "International Bestseller" are no less compelling. The cover price is pretty important too, as are money-off stickers, three-for-two decals and similar retailer contributions to the overall aesthetic.

On every possible count, Harry Potter covers score highly. The series design is consistent yet complementary; the blurbs by satisfied kiddie customers in *Chamber of Secrets* are a stroke of bookselling genius; the titles involve intriguing variations on an inviolate, well nigh iconic, word order; the depictions of Harry and co. differ from country to country, thereby adding to the collectability quotient; and retail prices vary tremendously, which brings out the bargain hunters big time. What's more, the American cover art, designed by Mary GrandPré, has attracted much favourable comment, even from otherwise sceptical academicians.

Content. Successful genre fiction, according to Palmer's classic study, relies on a combination of convention and invention.[6] Stories must be simultaneously familiar and different, in so far as they should adhere to the genre-savvy expectations of the readership yet go beyond seemingly established boundaries to newly imagined literary territory.

In this regard, the Harry Potter books are once again superlative. They brilliantly mix the stereotypical with the innovative. They not only combine several long-established literary genres – the boarding-school story, the coming-of-age story, the fantasy-world story, the good-versus-evil story – but introduce all sorts of entirely original touches, such as Quidditch, Diagon Alley, *The Daily Prophet*, brand-name broomsticks, and celebrity wizards like Gilderoy Lockhart. Each book in the series, furthermore, complies with this convention–invention dialectic. The component parts of the Harry Potter "formula" are unfailingly in place (the Dursleys, Hogwarts Express, the school year, the House Cup, the Hagrid sideshow, the villainy of Lord Voldemort), but the elements are rearranged, reworked or given a rest on each separate occasion.

Interest. Approximately 100,000 books are published each year in the United Kingdom. In the United States, it's 175,000 or thereabouts. The world total is somewhere in the region of a million. That's more than 2,500 titles per day: one every thirty seconds.[7] Markets don't come any more cut-throat. And it follows that in order to stand out from the massive me-too crowd, books must attract attention, build buzz and incite interest. Interest is all. Stimulating interest, if truth be told, is much more important than the literary merit of a book. Content is critical, but chatter closes the sale.

Clearly, when it comes to solving the interest = sales equation, Joanne Rowling is the Stephen Hawking of kid lit. Hell, she's Robert Boyle, Charles Darwin and Isaac Newton all rolled into one. As we'll see later, when the so-called *Goblet of Hype* gets the once-over, generating interest depends on yet another book marketing acronym: CHAT. This commences with a *Countdown*, where the days left until publication date are ostentatiously deducted on dedicated websites and in bookstore window displays. *Hints* are then dropped about the storyline, character development and – hold the front page! – impending deaths. An unfortunate *Accident* usually occurs with a couple of weeks to go, when pre-release copies of the strictly embargoed tome are stolen, hijacked, discovered in dumpsters or found on sale in unnamed Wal-Marts in deepest West Virginia. Finally, the big day arrives: *Ta-ra!* Ta-ra, needless to say, has an acronym all to itself, in Harry's case OTT: *Opening* bookshops at a minute after midnight; *Theme* parties in apt locations such as King's Cross station; and copious *TV* coverage of the unfolding first-day frenzy.

Obtainability. Nested acronyms may be the best-kept secret of book brand-builders, but there's more to selling tales than logophilia. Obtainability is essential. There are so many competing titles in the system these days that getting distribution is vital. Shelf space is limited, even in mega bookstores and especially in supermarkets, which have become one of the biggest bookselling outlets (Tesco accounted for 48 percent of *Goblet's* UK paperback sales). Hotspots within retail outlets, such as window displays, foyers and cash desks, are no less sought after. So much so that leading bookshops can command premium rates for their prime in-store real estate. And many do.

Harry Potter, suffice it to say, is unencumbered by shelf-space restrictions. Most stores have special sections devoted to the patron saint of booksellers – sections that magically expand to fill the entire establishment when a new title arrives. More amazing still is Harry's first-day trick of increasing the total number of bookselling establishments full stop. When the *Goblet of Fire* was unleashed, for instance, it was on sale in every imaginable outlet, from filling stations and fast-food franchises to factory shops and funfairs. A few even fell off the back of articulated lorries.[8]

Paradoxically, Harry owes at least some of his obtainability to unobtainability. That is to say, one of the things that kick-started the phenomenon was an initial product shortage. The print run of the first UK edition of *Philosopher's Stone* was 500 copies, which was perfectly normal for a kid-lit newcomer but proved totally inadequate as the buzz burgeoned. However, the very fact that the book was hard to obtain made its acquisition all the more urgent, not least because possession bestowed considerable schoolyard cachet on successful Harryhounds. Denial, as Bloomsbury discovered almost by accident, is an extremely powerful pocketbook emptier – an industrial-strength vacuum cleaner, almost – and every subsequent volume has come wrapped in dark hints about demand exceeding supply, insufficient copies to go around, gotta get it right away or you'll condemn your kids to unendurable ridicule. Meanwhile, the world's printing presses are working at full capacity and the global stock of stockrooms is brimming with copies of Rowling's latest release. Bloomsbury's such a tease...

ACCIO, ACCIO, ACCIO

Teasing the customer is a sure-fire marketing strategy, as I'll explain in due course (or possibly not; it depends how I feel at the time). However, Harry Potter has a final acronymic trick up his sleeve. There's more to ACCIO than embeds. It's recursive as well. ACCIO loops back on itself like a bookbiz oroboros. Pottermania is a perpetual promotion machine where each storytelling element fuels the PR fire and the PR fire further fuels the PR fire. Not only is Harry Potter marketed, the *marketing* of Harry Potter is marketed. When each book launch comes round – be it soft cover, clothbound, special edition or completely new title – the hawking of Harry forms part of the story.

This selling story, it must be stressed, is not a sideshow. It is central to the whole Potter phenomenon. One of the mainsprings of Harry's US take-off, for example, was the sale of the American rights for an unprecedented six-figure sum.[9] The scale of Scholastic's outlay attracted an enormous amount of media interest – interest in the author (who's worth such an amount?), interest in the outcome (will sales justify the spend?), interest in the story (a British boarding school, you say?), interest in the mechanics of recouping the advance (how on earth will Scholastic sell the thing?) Interest, in other words, that would have been withheld from a less risky publishing venture, interest that served to spread the word and build a buzz, interest that helped ensure Scholastic's gamble paid off.

Volume 1, furthermore, was just the start of the ACCIO inferno. An especially interesting aspect of release-date frenzy, for books 4 and 5 in particular, is the prominent part played by statistical screamers. Newspaper articles and television programmes are riddled with staggering marketing factoids (see table). Number of copies sold! Sizes of print runs! First-day sales figures! Pre-publication orders at Amazon.com! Behind-the-scenes logistical support! Price comparisons among competing retailers! Hot Harrystats from hither, yon and the

PHOENIX FACTOIDS

- Bloomsbury's share price promptly rose by £8.45 when the manuscript was delivered on 15 January 2003.

- The book has 766 pages and is more than 255,000 words long. It weighs 1.3 kg (2.8 lb).

- It was launched simultaneously in Britain, the United States, Canada, Australia and other countries in an English edition.

- After the publishing date was announced on 15 January 2003, Amazon took more than 1.1 million advance orders with 400,000 in the UK alone, making it the most pre ordered book in history thus far.

- About 8.5 million copies of the book were shipped to the US.

- British libraries ordered 11,000 advance copies.

- Tesco opened 367 stores across the UK at 00.01 a.m. on Saturday 21 June 2003. Half of all UK copies of the *Goblet* paperback were sold by Tesco in the week of release. Tesco's website received more than 50,000 pre-orders for *Phoenix*.

- Asda ordered 500,000 copies of the book and each of its 260 stores gave 10 books to local schools.

- J. K. Rowling made approximately £30m from the book.

- Prior to *Phoenix, Harry Potter and the Goblet of Fire* was the fastest selling book in history; 372,000 copies were sold on the first weekend of publication in July 2000.

Sources: *Guardian*, 21 June 2003, p. 3; *The Times*, 21 June 2003, p. 9.

rest of the civilized world!! This just in: Potter is the first English-language title to feature on France's foremost bestsellers list!!!

True or not, accurate or otherwise, amply padded or conveniently plucked from thin air, there's no denying the rhetorical power of gee-whiz, super-duper marketing factlets. They have an inherent wow factor, a *Guinness Book of World Records* quality, an echo of P. T. Barnum's Greatest Show on Earth, that can't fail to impress neutral observers or, for that matter, shame even the most sceptical Potterphobe into submission. There's a reader born every minute, as P. T. Barnum almost said.

Above and beyond Barnumism, the real beauty of the Harry Potter book brand, from a marketing perspective, is that the statistics 'n' stuff become ever more impressive, ever more amazing, ever more unbelievable with every publishing occasion. Heaven only knows what they'll look like when the final volume comes round. Personally, I'm waiting for the day when they compare Harry Potter to humanity's place in the universal scheme of things, from Big Bang to 2005. You know, the one where they claim that if all time were compressed into a single day, the dinosaurs would've died around teatime, humankind crawled out of the primordial swamp at ten minutes to midnight, and writing was invented with a couple of seconds to go. I can just see it now: if time began with "Mr and Mrs Dursley," the first words of the first volume, Harry Potter himself hit town on the full stop after "scar," which we already know is the final word of the final book. Makes you think, doesn't it?

I CAN'T BELIEVE IT'S NOT PROFIT

Only a nerd, I'm sure you've concluded, could possibly come up with something like that. Appropriately, our final acronym – the one that accounts for all the above numerical rhetoric – is SAD. SAD squared, in fact. SAD^2 works as follows: Sales Statistics generate Amazement, which generates Anticipation, which generates Desire, which generates Demand, which duly adds to the Sales Statistics, which generate additional Amazement, which generates increased Anticipation, which generates insatiable Desire, which generates uncontrollable Demand, which duly adds to the staggering Sales Statistics . . . and so the Rowling road rolls ever on.

The ultimate irony, nevertheless, is that many bookshops make little or no profit from the HP sales detonation.[10] Competition is so tough for the Potter pound that booksellers cut their prices to the quick and in some cases – Tesco, for example – sell the teenage mage as a loss leader. The bestselling books in history are thus costing the marketing system millions, and the more books sold the more the system loses, at least in theory. Even anti-capitalists can buy Harry Potter with confidence. The boy wonder's got something for everyone.

Wizard, or what?

The Cinema Story

Nobody really knows which films will be big. There are no sure-fire commercial ideas any more. Nobody knows anything in the movie business because no one can predict popular taste.

William Goldman

YOU'RE GOING TO NEED A BIGGER BOOKSTORE

A couple of years back, I was living in the United States, the land of the free gift and home of the brand portfolio. As I travelled round the country, giving lectures on Harry Potter to serious scholarly audiences who cared little for tyro wizards and even less for marketing researchers interested in such trivialities, I made a point of dropping into the biggest bookstore in town. Not to check out the Harry Potter situation, you understand, just to see if my own books were in stock.

On stumbling tearfully for the exits, I couldn't help but notice that the boy wizard was everywhere. There were dedicated Harry Potter departments, huge in-store displays and all manner of mementoes, from calendars and address books to action figures and cuddly toys. That much I expected, since the fourth book had been released six months earlier. What surprised me was that most of the merchandise was on sale: 50 percent off; Harry Potter clear-out; Dark Mark mark-downs; two for the price of one all over the shop. I even came across a guide to Harry Potter discount merchandise that was itself deeply discounted.

Naturally, I concluded that the Potter fad had run its course. The golden goose had been overworked by bookbiz battery farms, and its gilded yield was falling. The golden calf had been lassoed, branded and unceremoniously slaughtered by the literary cowpokes at Scholastic's Seventh Avenue corral. Or something like that.

My impression, needless to say, was mistaken. I had failed to take a crucial factor into account: Hollywood. Just like the

Seventh Cavalry, Warner Brothers' platoon of Prada-clad ponytails was riding to the rescue of a temporarily beleaguered brand. True, some Pottermanes saw this cinematic intervention as a Wounded Knee waiting to happen, but it can't be denied that when it comes to blowing a brand bugle or mounting a marketing charge, there's nothing to compare with Hollywood Boulevard's rough riders.[1]

YOU TOLKIEN TO ME?

Commentators on Harry Potter books spend an inordinate amount of time identifying the roots of Rowling's writing. The antecedents of her series are endlessly speculated on and raked over. JKR, in fairness, has never denied or downplayed her literary influences, which include just about everything from Jane Austen to Richard Adams.[2] To my knowledge, however, she has never acknowledged cinema's influence on her writing, though we know she was an avid film-goer during her years at Exeter University.

Yet anyone who's ever bought a megabucket of popcorn, or chugged a big gulp serving of soda, can see that the cinema is in there, too. The memory-erasing charms are less than a million miles from *Men in Black*; the time-turning denouement of *Azkaban* is not uninfluenced by *Back to the Future*; the animated household appliances are reminiscent of Disney's *Beauty and the Beast*; the Avada Kedavra curse echoes and evokes *The Lion King's* Hakuna Matata; the flying Ford Anglia in *Secrets* is *ET* to a T; the titular construction "Harry Potter and the Whatever of Wherever" isn't so much a homage to the Indiana Jones sequels as a Xerox. Many, moreover, have noted the series' debt to the *Star Wars* saga, Luke and Darth's relationship in particular. What, after all, is Hagrid but Chewbacca with speech therapy?

In addition to the admittedly minor influence of blockbuster movies – I'll start to get worried when Harry's alone in a lift-shaft, whupping Voldemort's minions, wearing a Bruce Willisish T-shirt and wielding the Yippy-ki-aye curse – the series also contains tinctures of several UK television programmes. Mundungus Fletcher is within spitting distance of Del Boy Trotter, the much-loved anti-hero of *Only Fools and Horses*. The expression "He who must not be named" brings *Rumpole of the Bailey* to mind.[3] Gilderoy Lockhart is a latter-day reincarnation of *Blackadder's* Lord Flasheart, near enough, and some of the author's locutions are unadulterated Rowan Atkinson ("mimblewimble," "blibbering," "mimbulus mimbletonia"). Such is the influence of television that adverts occasionally get a walk-on part, most notably Schweppes' "you know who." Still, it could've been a lot worse. Rowling could have included "The World's Favourite Wizard," "Beans Means Botts," "Just Floo It," "Durmstrang durch Technik," "You should have gone to Spellsavers," "I Can't Believe It's Not Butterbeer" and many more besides.

I LOVE THE SMELL OF NIFFLERS IN THE MORNING

Now, none of this detracts from J. K. Rowling's astonishing achievements. All authors borrow from their peers, predecessors and popular culture. As T. S. Eliot famously confessed, "Immature poets imitate; mature poets steal."[4] What it *does* demonstrate is the vividness of Rowling's imagination. There's a powerful visual component to the books. The original manuscript of *Philosopher's Stone* was illustrated with some of Jo's own drawings, though these failed to make the final cut. It is no exaggeration to state that the first book reads like a series of Spielbergian storyboards: the opening of Diagon Alley is akin to that scene in *Jurassic Park* where the dinosaurs first appear; the ride through the bowels of Gringotts is similar to the mineshaft sequence in *Indiana Jones and the Temple of Doom;* crossing the lake to a light-speckled Hogwarts could be an editing suite outtake from *Close Encounters;* and the three tests en route to the chamber containing the titular stone bring back memories of *Indiana Jones and the Last Crusade.*

To be sure, the first book is much more than a mere Spielberg pastiche. It fits perfectly into the twelve-stage story trajectory that structures numerous successful movies including *Titanic, Unforgiven, Pretty Woman* and *O Brother, Where Art Thou?* (see text panel). Predicated on Joseph Campbell's much-vaunted monomyth, as revamped for the cinematic community by Christopher Vogler, this commences with an Ordinary World setting (the Dursley household is "perfectly normal, thank you very much"), continues with a Call to Action (Harry's avalanche of letters from Hogwarts), culminates in a Supreme Ordeal (Potter's struggle with Quirrell for the Philosopher's Stone) and concludes with an older and wiser protagonist's return to the

THE TWELVE STAGES OF THE *PHILOSOPHER'S STONE*

Ordinary World: Harry Potter lives in an anonymous British suburb, Little Whinging, Surrey. An orphan with an unusual scar on his forehead, he is maltreated by his relatives, Vernon and Petunia Dursley, and bullied by his corpulent cousin, Dudley.

Call to Adventure: Just prior to his eleventh birthday, Harry receives a letter from "no one." It is confiscated and destroyed by Uncle Vernon. Further letters flood into the Dursley household.

Refusal of Call: The family flees the torrent of letters and take refuge in a shack on an isolated island. A hairy giant bursts in and informs Harry that he has a place at Hogwarts School of Witchcraft and Wizardry. Uncle Vernon tries to withhold his consent, but soon thinks better of it.

Meeting with the Mentor: Hagrid, the hairy giant, carries Harry off and introduces him to the magic world, where he is known as "the boy who lived." It seems he survived a childhood encounter with an evil wizard, Lord Voldemort, though his parents paid the ultimate price.

Crossing the First Threshold: In quick succession, Harry is introduced to the wizard's shopping street, Diagon Alley; platform 9¾ at King's Cross station; the Hogwarts Express, an old-fashioned steam train; the magical Hogwarts School itself; and the Sorting Hat, which places him in Gryffindor House, like his parents before him.

Tests, Allies, Enemies: Harry makes friends with fellow Gryffindors Ron Weasley and Hermione Granger; runs afoul of the Slytherins;

Ordinary World (Harry goes back to the Dursleys, armed with new-found magical knowledge).[5] Granted, the concluding stages are rather more compressed than is normal in Tinseltown, but as the book is the first in a series of seven this is only to be expected.

discovers that he has a natural gift for Quidditch, a kind of airborne polo; and struggles with his classwork, Potions in particular.

Approach to the Inmost Cave: Harry, Hermione and Ron realize that the mysterious Philosopher's Stone is hidden in the school, where it is protected by Fluffy, a fearsome three-headed dog. They solve three riddles en route to the secret chamber where the stone is stored.

Supreme Ordeal: Alone, Harry struggles with Quirrell, a two-faced schoolteacher desperate to acquire the stone for his master, the villainous Lord Voldemort, who is trying to make a comeback, as evil wizards are wont to do.

Reward: The stone magically appears in Harry's pocket, and in the ensuing struggle, Harry realizes that his touch is death to the Quirrell–Voldemort combo. He holds on for grim life.

The Road Back: Harry wakes up in the hospital wing. The headmaster, Albus Dumbledore, had come to his rescue and carried him back to safety. Dumbledore explains why the stone appeared in his pocket, why Lord Voldemort requires it and the likelihood of the evil one's return.

Resurrection: Even though Harry and his pals have broken school rules, Dumbledore awards them extra house points that are sufficient to pip Slytherin and win Gryffindor the house cup for the first time in seven years.

Return with the Elixir: Harry and his school chums return on the Hogwarts Express to London, where he is met by the dreadful Dursleys. Although the apprentice wizard isn't permitted to use magic outside school grounds, the Dursleys don't know that. Payback time, Dudley.

It doesn't stop there, either. The books become increasingly cinematic as the series progresses. The inclusion of subplots and flashbacks (*Azkaban*); the introduction of spectacular James Bondoid opening sequences (*Goblet*); climactic *Star Wars*-style duels with wands instead of light sabres (*Goblet*); and, above all, the shoot-em-up denouement of *Phoenix*, where Dumbledore and Voldemort go magus-à-magus in the Ministry of Magic, are piped from that inexhaustible storytelling aquifer under Studio City.[6]

When all is said and done, the books embody the "small guy against overwhelming odds" archetype that is the pre-eminent trope in modern American cinema. *Rocky, Rambo, Gladiator, Braveheart, Seabiscuit, High Noon, Die Hard, Dodgeball, Kingpin, Taxi Driver, Jerry Maguire, Mission Impossible, Independence Day, Dog Day Afternoon, High Plains Drifter, On the Waterfront, A Fistful of Dollars, All the President's Men, The Magnificent Seven, The Untouchables, The Adventures of Robin Hood*, to name but a few, are the cinematic headwaters of Harry Potter. It is no exaggeration to state that this David versus Goliath scenario is the primal narrative of the United States; the country was founded on it. As such, Rowling's staggering Stateside success should come as no surprise; nor should the abiding interest of the Dream Factory's production controllers.

IN ST MUNGO'S NO ONE CAN HEAR YOU SCREAM

Although the first book finally hit the world's cinema screens a full four years after it was published, the movie rights were in play within a few weeks of its appearance. The printing presses were still cooling down when Christopher Little let it be known that he'd been approached by two Hollywood studios and one independent American producer. We'll probably never know whether these approaches were kosher. Perhaps such claims are standard industry practice, the agency equivalent of pump-priming coins in a panhandler's tin cup. What we do know is that a Warner Brothers scout, David Heyman, was the first serious bidder. With the encouragement of his HP-addicted children ringing in his ears, as well as the enthusiasm of fellow Heyday executive Tanya Seghatchian, he sought to secure an option on the hot Potter property.

Aside from its obvious filmic elements, the book was just about as tasty a bone as ever is thrown in Tinseltown's direction. As a possible seven-part series, it was a money-spinning franchise in the making, a veritable McDonald's of the multiplexes. The characters were very "toyetic," what's more, which would have Mattel et al. slavering for a slice of the action figures. And the target market for the property was smack-bang in the middle of the movie business sweet spot, tweenagers of all ages. It is little wonder that Little was soon under siege.

The great literary agent was not to be rushed, however, and more than two years passed before the Warners deal was done and dusted. By that stage, Rowling had been catapulted from poverty-stricken single parent to one of the world's bestselling authors. This not only changed the balance of negotiating power considerably but guaranteed a ready-made audience for the films and ancillaries.

There's a world of difference, nevertheless, between developing a franchise and making it work. Accordingly, the two years between doing the WB deal and delivering the first instalment to the megaplexes were filled with almost as much drama as the dramatizations themselves – drama that was played out in the full glare of front-page publicity.

First up was the drama surrounding the director. The sainted Steven Spielberg was very interested at one stage, but Rowling's fears that he'd Americanize, sentimentalize and generally Spielbergize her Spielbergian creation meant that the director's chair went elsewhere. Warner Brothers organized a directorial beauty contest for the honour of helming Harry, and after casting their eyes over several prominent candidates including Alan Parker, Brad Silberling, Ivan Reitman and Terry Gilliam, they entrusted the franchise to Christopher Columbus. Director of *Home Alone* and *Mrs Doubtfire* among other kiddie classics, Columbus was regarded as a safe pair of hands. A property of this potential magnitude can't be messed with, you must appreciate, as countless collapsed "tent-pole projects" bear sorry witness.[7]

Next up was the script. At 223 pages, *Harry Potter and the Philosopher's Stone* is the shortest of the books, yet it's far too long for a screenplay, which typically averages 120 double-spaced pages. On top of the unavoidable downsizing and all the difficult editorial decisions this involved, the "source writer" was determined to protect her creation. A self-confessed control freak, and no doubt cognizant of Hollywood's philistine propensity to mutilate much-loved works of literature, Rowling relinquished precious profit points in order to ensure that there weren't too many slips 'twixt script and screen. Fortunately, she hit it off with Steve

Cloves, the hot-shot screenwriter behind *Wonder Boys,* who was diplomatic enough to tell Rowling that Hermione was his favourite character. Quite.

I COULDA BEEN A DEMENTOR

A script is one thing; its realization is something else entirely. And once again, Rowling used her clout to ensure that the $125 million movie was made in Britain, with an all-British cast and crew. 'Ere long, many a UK dinner party spent many an enchanted evening playing fantasy casting calls. Robbie Coltrane was a universal shoo-in for Hagrid; Snape was surely written with Alan Rickman in mind; Dumbledore, McGonagall and Mrs Weasley were filled, to everyone's instant approval, by Richard Harris, Maggie Smith and Julie Walters respectively. But what of the leads? In classic *Gone With the Wind* fashion, the producers launched a massive nationwide search for the boy who'd play the boy who lived. Thousands applied, the producers despaired, and then, in a moment of pure movie magic – magic utterly untainted by PR personages familiar with the Lauren Bacall/Sean Connery/Michelle Pfeiffer discovery narrative – Daniel Radcliffe was spotted in a West End theatre one star-crossed night. His parents stoutly resisted the call of the klieg lights, even though Daniel had appeared in several previous productions. Then it turned out that he shared a birthday with Jo Rowling and Harry Potter. A clear case of cinematic kismet. Sorry, did I say kismet? I meant claptrap.

Shooting began at Leavesden studios in September 2000, with additional location work at such suitably photogenic settings as Alnwick Castle and Gloucester Cathedral. No sooner had it started than the buzz-builders set to work. Websites, chat rooms, movie magazines and so forth were salted with tantalizing nuggets of on-set information: stills, storyboards, progress reports and "watch this space" come-ons. When the first trailer was released in April 2001, it made the main evening news on both sides of the Atlantic and enjoyed hectares of priceless press coverage. It even carried an iffy Warner Brothers comedy, *See Spot Run*, to the top of the US box office as people coughed up their $7 just to see the appended Potter images. A second teaser trailer was issued in June, and it too triggered a frenzy of downloading and cyberchatter. Better yet, the movie was going head to head with the first instalment of the *Lord of the Rings* trilogy, which added a delicious "battle of the blockbusters" sizzle to the discussions. There's nothing like a little phoney rivalry to add millions to admissions.

By the time the red-carpeted premieres came around in early November, *Harry Potter and the Philosopher's/Sorcerer's Stone* had been apotheosized into a kind of post-9/11 balm for the western world. Despite sniffy reviews of the too long, too ponderous, too true to the books tenor, especially in America, the movie did the business. Aided and abetted by a $40 million marketing spend – TV ads, radio spots, press inserts, mega-billboards, website freebies, promotional giveaways, Times Square Jumbotron and suchlike – the boy wizard barnstormed the box office. Opening on an unprecedented

3,672 US screens, it broke the first-day record ($31 million), the weekend record ($93 million), the seven-day record ($130 million) and almost every box office record thereafter. When all the ticket stubs were counted and Hollywood's accounting imagineers had worked their magic on the receipts, *Harry Potter and the Philosopher's/Sorcerer's Stone* had garnered a worldwide gross of $967 million, second only to *Titanic* on the all-time list. An unsinkable franchise had been successfully launched, with nary an iceberg in sight.

The cinematic voyage continued with *Harry Potter and the Chamber of Secrets* (budget $120 million, marketing $50 million, director Christopher Columbus, released November 2002, worldwide gross $877 million); *Harry Potter and the Prisoner of Azkaban* (budget $130 million, marketing $50 million, director Alfonso Cuarón, released June 2004, worldwide gross $789); and *Harry Potter and the Goblet of Fire* (budget $130 million, director Mike Newell, due for release 18 November 2005).[8] Like the books, the movies adhere to the "same only different" offering that is the essence of generic cultural forms: same set-up, with different elements; same characters, with different arrivals; same cast, with different faces; same crew, with different directors; same buzz-building, with different discussion points; same release patterns, with different gee-whiz statistics; same reviews, with different nits picked; same consumer response, with different top-line figures; same DVD, soundtrack and television licensing deals, which have earned an estimated $750 million thus far.[9] The grosses are sliding, admittedly, which is unusual for blockbuster movies, but unless a point is reached where production costs exceed revenue streams, the good ship Potter will continue to cruise across the storm-tossed waters of the box-office briney.[10]

I'LL BE BLACK

It's easy to criticize the Harry Potter films. And many have availed themselves of the opportunity. Daniel Radcliffe's performance, for example, was once unfairly described as "hewn from the adamantine oaks of the Forbidden Forest."[11] The special effects, furthermore, are less than special and far from effective, the Quidditch scenes especially. However, it's hard to argue with the second biggest box-office take of all time, and even harder to belittle Rowling's tenacity. The movies are exceptionally true to the books, a fact attributable in no small measure to her resolute stance on what's acceptable and what isn't. Given that "source writers" are the lowest form of life in Hollywood's pecking order, given the liberties that the Dream Factory ordinarily takes with works of literature, and given that Jo had no previous experience of dealing with the Death Eaters of La-La Land, her achievement is really quite astonishing. It's not every day that a movie rookie strikes out Steven Spielberg, much less disses Dreamworks' major-domo. At the Scottish premiere of *Philosopher's Stone*, Rowling praised Columbus's fidelity to the sacred text and quipped, "Thank God it wasn't Spielberg." This was quickly followed by, "Do you think we could be sued for that?"

Be that as it may, Rowling's ostensible defeat of the Burbank basilisks is less clear-cut than it seems. It's important to appreciate that, from a movie-marketing perspective, it's often helpful to have a critic on board. This is especially so when the property is precious, delicate or cherished, as is the case with HP. Rowling's much-trumpeted determination to resist Hollywoodization is a powerful marketing tool, since it authenticates, legitimizes and ultimately sanctions the production (Jo says it's OK, so it must be OK). Rowling's a brand guardian, and the existence of a brand guardian is, in purely promotional terms, a necessary guarantee of quality.

Hollywood, don't forget, is not above criticizing itself in order to make the sale. *Jurassic Park* is a condemnation of the theme-park industry – one that conveniently spawned several theme-park rides – and actually features the tie-in merchandise in the movie itself. *Waterworld* is a paean to the preservation of the earth's resources, a paean that squandered some $200 million in production costs and only just covered its outlay at the box office. The ostentatious critique of movie merchandising in Disney's *Hercules* isn't so much tongue-in-cheek as two fingers down the throat. And then, of course, there's *Shrek 2*...[12]

ROUND UP THE USUAL SLYTHERINS

Again, none of this means that Rowling is an unwitting stooge for the Steven Spielbergs of this world, although I suspect that had the franchise fallen at the first hurdle, blame would have been heaped on interfering outsiders who know nothing about the movie industry. What it *does* mean is that cinematic pearls sometimes need a piece of grit in the movie-marketing oyster. And whatever their artistic merits, there's no denying that the Harry Potter movies are pearls where it really matters. In the multiplexes du monde.

That said, there is an ever-widening chasm between the creator's utterances and the cinematic experiences. When she says, as she invariably does, that the special effects are spectacular, extraordinary, or "Just how I imagined Quidditch to be," she is losing credibility with the people who buy the tickets. Sympathisers may surmise that she obviously doesn't get out to the cinema very often these days. But sceptics see this as a sell-out to the PR/talk show/*Hello* magazine constituency, where every movie is the best of the best, remaining on message is the immutable MO, and pigs not only fly in perfect formation but perform aerobatics to boot.

Keeping Rowling on message is an elementary marketing mistake, however. Her criticisms are proof that the franchise isn't beholden to crass commercial considerations. She should be encouraged to carp at the cinematic product next time round. That'll pack them in for certain. They'll be so keen to see what's got JK's proverbials in a twist that all previous records will snap like elastic.

Here's looking at you, Hermione.

6

The Secrets Story

The customer is always right, even
if fatally stupid and misguided.

The Economist

TEASE PLEASE

If there is one word that encapsulates the peddling of Harry Potter, that word is *tease*. The merest glance at Joanne Rowling's award-winning website reveals that teasing the customer is her preferred marketing method. Tricks, puzzles, mysteries, red herrings, supposedly secret rooms and all the riddling rest are sprinkled liberally throughout the site, which she writes herself. She drops hints about the outcome of the saga, the fate of individual characters, the clues contained in various episodes and the significance of forthcoming book titles ("I can't reveal the title of the final book. My publisher would kill me!"). What's more, she torments her readers with the ultimate questions: Who's for the chop? Can Harry survive? Is Ron a goner? Dumbledore's doomed, isn't he? Will a bit wizard whack Hagrid?

And she's not alone. Taking their lead from Joanne, Harry's handlers go out of their way to torment customers. In the nicest possible way, naturally. The Philosopher's Stone DVD, for instance, contains numerous hidden scenes that can be accessed only via a cryptic combination of clicks on the bricks of the back wall of the Leaky Cauldron. In the computer games, the grounds of Hogwarts are seething with secrets, subtle hints, concealed clues and what have you. None of this is unusual in computer gaming or extras-enhanced DVDs, admittedly, but it is particularly conspicuous in the Harry Potter franchise, where most tie-ins involve tricks and puzzles of one kind or another. Another aspect of the same teasing ethos is good old-fashioned denial marketing. That is, making life difficult for the customer, thereby increasing his or her desire to acquire the merchandise in question. Denial relies on the elemental marketing principle that people want what they can't have, and the less they can have it, the more they want it. This primordial psychological premise – what Germans term *Torschlusspanik*, the fear of doors closing – is employed by exclusive nightclubs (impossible to get in), top-notch restaurants (try again next year), high-end retail outlets (not for the likes of you), to-die-for West End shows (tickets are so hot they spontaneously combust) and individually customized superbrands (only the best need apply, and there's a waiting list for the waiting list). It is equally evident at the bottom-feeding end of the marketing spectrum, where sales pitches like "last few days", "limited time only", "hurry while stocks last," and "the Lego Hogwarts Castle kit won't be in until after Christmas," are well-nigh ubiquitous.[2]

DENIED!

Marketease, moreover, was standard practice in Hollywood before the blockbuster revolution. Whereas today's mega-movies open wide, with a view to generating massive first-weekend grosses that are then used to publicize the movie further and give it legs, old-time movie marketers often restricted availability in order to lengthen lines, increase interest, inculcate a must-see mentality among cinemagoers and generate the all-important Big Mo (momentum). When *Jaws* was set for release in 1975, it was booked into a then record 900 theatres. The legendary head of Universal Studios,

Lew Wasserman, promptly dropped 300 of them in order to foment the frenzy. "I want this picture to play all summer long," he said. "I don't want people in Palm Springs to see the picture in Palm Springs. I want them to get in their cars and drive to Hollywood."[3]

And they did.

Such movie-marketing tactics are rarely used nowadays, more's the pity, but when Christopher Columbus claimed that Chamber of Secrets was way too scary for younger children, arachnophobes especially, he was treading the time-worn path of tantalization. Nothing is more guaranteed to get children excited than the suggestion that a film's too frightening for them. No doubt the same don't-go-there tactic will be employed when Goblet of Fire is released. It features the death of a key character! The kids might be traumatized!! Cue stampede to the box office!!!

Rowling's much-publicized doubts about meretricious merchandising work in a similar way. When she urges parents not to buy certain products, as she often does, she's merely adding to the items' intrigue and thereby increasing customer interest, arousal, desire and ultimately acquisitiveness ("if Jo doesn't like it, it must be worth investigating\investing in."). Her say in what goes memorabilia-wise is a boon to Warner Brothers as well, since Jo's possible disapproval can be deployed when negotiating with would-be licensees. The threat of incurring JK's wrath is a powerful weapon that can be used to beat suppliers down on price or any other negotiable (superior quality, better delivery, promotional support, you name it).[4]

TEASE BOOKS ARE MADE FOR HAWKING

The quintessence of Potterease, nevertheless, is secreted among the book marketers. Although denial-based bookselling strategies are nothing new – the anti-marketing of books began in 1967, when Harper & Row refused to release review copies of William Manchester's The Death of the President and the ensuing publicity propelled it to number one on the New York Times bestseller list' – there's no denying that Bloomsbury and Scholastic are modern masters of tantalizing, teasing and tormentation.

The marketing strategy for Goblet of Fire, for example, involved a complete blackout on advance information. It started with a teaser campaign consisting of "Harry's Back" posters and a countdown to the rapidly approaching publication date. However, the title, pagination and price were kept secret until two weeks before the big day. Review copies were withheld, author interviews were prohibited and foreign translations deferred for fear of injudicious leaks. Juicy plot details, including the death of a (minor) character and Harry's sexual awakening, were drip-fed to a slavering press corps immediately prior to the launch. It was even announced, with some solemnity, that the original manuscript had been locked in a carefully guarded safe after it was almost stolen from under a Bloomsbury executive's nose. Gasp! Shock! Don't these people keep back-up copies on disks?

Printers and distributors, meantime, were required to sign strict, legally enforceable confidentiality agreements.

Bookstores were bound by a ruthlessly policed embargo, though they were allowed to display the tantalizing tome (in locked cages) for a brief period in the run-up to Harry Potter Day, 8 July 2000. Fake television footage of heavily armoured security vans delivering the precious Potter cargo to online booksellers was also produced and broadcast a week before publication. Twenty advance copies of the top-secret book were "accidentally" sold by The Supermarket That Must Not Be Named and one of the "lucky" children was miraculously tracked down by the world's press and splashed across every front page worth its salt. Another copy "inexplicably" landed on the news desk of the Scottish Daily Record, though it was returned unopened to the publisher by the paper's noble newshounds. Curiously, the story of the accident – and the journalists' righteous response – somehow found its way to the front pages. Only a cynic would infer that the incident was prearranged.

The Order of the Phoenix strategy followed a broadly similar pattern, albeit with even tighter restrictions this time round. Scholastic's stealth campaign, as Beahm notes, included: no review copies; no book signings; no media coverage, bar one BBC and one NBC television interview; the trusty countdown clocks on the publishers' websites; and the by now traditional midnight opening fandango. Deliveries to bookstores came in special tamper-proof boxes featuring ostentatiously opaque wrapping and overprinted with the magic marketing words, "Do not open before 21 June 2003."[6] Still, the best stunt of all was pulled by J. K. Rowling herself on launch day. Just after midnight, she

88

turned up unannounced at Waterstones in Edinburgh, and started signing copies for stunned kiddie customers. Pandemonium ensued. PRmonium swiftly followed.

HARRY POTTER PRICKED A PECK OF PICKLED Ps

It is arguable, I grant you, that the author is more of a beneficiary than an instigator of Bloomsbury's and Scholastic's marketeasing. The evidence nevertheless suggests that Rowling is the guiding spirit, not least because the teasing didn't really begin until the third book, when Jo became conscious of Harry's marketing clout, and only took off with book 4, by which time Potter was the hottest marketing property on the planet. As noted previously, it is not in an author's professional interest to flaunt her sales ability, let alone her self-promotional prowess.

Yet regardless of who was responsible for what, the evidence in Phoenix is irrefutable. Rowling is not only conscious of marketease but uses it as a fundamental narrative device. The antagonist of Phoenix, devious Dolores Umbridge, is undermined by a masterpiece of denial marketing when her attempts to spread disinformation about the boy wizard are thwarted. Upset by the High Inquisitor's insinuations, Harry tells his side of the story to Rita Skeeter, the hackette nonpareil. When the piece is duly splashed across the front cover of The Quibbler, acting headmistress Umbridge makes the mistake of banning the periodical. But far from killing the story, her act of denial merely piques people's curiosity, and in very short order her authority crumbles:

'What exactly are you so happy about?' Harry asked her.

'Oh, Harry, don't you see?' Hermione breathed. 'If she could have done one thing to make absolutely sure that every single person in the school will read your interview, it was banning it!'

And it seemed that Hermione was quite right. By the end of the day, though Harry had not seen so much of a corner of The Quibbler anywhere in the school, the whole place seemed to be quoting the interview to each other.

(Order of the Phoenix, p. 513)

Now, there's nothing like a ban to inflame consumption, as marketers of everything from Frankie Goes to Hollywood to The Passion of the Christ attest. Nevertheless, there's more to teasing than denial. Like so many marketing terms, TEASE is an acronym. Its five components are: Tricksterism, Exclusivity, Amplification, Secrecy and Entertainment.[7] Harry Potter epitomizes marketease. Tricks are repeatedly played on the public (Rowling's website, the "lucky" schoolkid). Exclusivity is actively practised (special limited editions in Ancient Greek, Latin and Gaelic) or cunningly alluded to ("drat, not enough copies to go round,"). Amplify, amplify, amplify is the publishers' byword, since everything that is remotely newsworthy is shovelled into the media's insatiable maw (the shovelling is also shovelled constantly). Secrecy, furthermore, is central to the whole operation in everything from the titles of forthcoming books to rumours of the deaths of major characters. The stories themselves are mysteries, remember; a judicious mix of Tom Brown and James Bond.

Above all, the Harry Potter phenomenon is enormously entertaining. The books are wonderfully entertaining. The reaction of the consuming public is incredibly entertaining. The reaction of the Harry-haters is entertaining too, as we shall see very shortly. And, needless to say, the marketing campaign itself is a wonderful example of promotional razzle-dazzle, hocus-pocus, hubba-hubba.

Marketese is the antithesis of conventional marketing, which aims to satisfy consumers' every conceivable whim. Giving people what they want, when they want it, at a price they are prepared to pay, is the basis of modern marketing. As marketing bases go, it goes very well indeed. It works. It has proved itself. It's all fine and dandy. It's not the only way to sell stuff, however. In truth, too much pandering to customers is unhealthy; it makes them harder and harder to satisfy, more and more demanding, less and less appreciative.[8]

FISHERMAN'S FRIEND

The conventional marketing approach, appropriately enough, reminds me of one of the Grimm Brothers' fairy tales, "The Fisherman and His Wife." A tad un-PC for today's taste, the tale tells of a fisherman who catches a flounder one day, an enchanted flounder that asks to be released. The kindly fisherman agrees, but when he tells his wife about his selfless act, she scolds him for failing to demand a wish in return. "What should I have wished for?" he asks. "Ah," says his wife, "Don't you think it's awful that we've got to keep living in such a hovel? It stinks and it's disgusting. You should have wished for a little cottage. Go back and call him. Tell him we want a little cottage. I'm sure he'll give us one."

The fisherman returns to the seashore, where he delivers the following oration:

Flounder, flounder in the sea,
If you're a man, then speak to me.
Though I do not care for my wife's request,
I've come to ask it nonetheless.

The flounder appears and grants his wish. When the fisherman gets back home, their hovel has been transformed into a cottage. However, his wife soon grows dissatisfied. She demands a castle instead of the cottage, and the fisherman goes back to the seashore, where he repeats his rhyme. The flounder reappears and does the needful. The same sequence of events duly transpires, only this time his wife demands to be king. King she becomes, with riches befitting her position:

There were sentries standing in front of the gate, along with many soldiers, drums and trumpets. When he entered the palace, he found that everything was made of pure marble and gold and had velvet covers with large golden tassels. The doors to the hall were opened, and he could see the whole court. His wife was sitting on a high throne of gold and diamonds, and on her head she had a big golden crown and in her hand a sceptre of pure gold and jewels. Two rows of ladies-in-waiting were standing on either side of her, each lady a head shorter than the next. The fisherman stepped forward and said,

'Oh, wife, now you're king aren't you?'

'Yes,' said his wife, 'now I am king.'

Still unsatisfied, she asks to be emperor. Granted. She
wants to be pope. Sorted. She wants to be like God, says the
fisherman to the flounder. Done. The fisherman returns home
and finds her living in a hovel once more.[9]
There's a lesson in there somewhere.

There is a non-reversed version of this chapter
online, if you need it (www.sfxbrown.com).

7

The Spin-offs Story

Did Prince Charles model his temple on Hagrid's cottage in Harry Potter?

Newspaper headline

O WARNER BROTHERS, WHERE ART THOU?

As a rule, I try not to buy Harry Potter tie-in merchandise. With three teenage girls in the family, all of whom are avid Potter fans, the temptation is always there, but the budget, unfortunately, isn't. A few years ago, what's more, we got caught up in the Lego Hogwarts Castle debacle, when stocks of the Christmas season's must-have toy were insufficient to meet consumer demand. No amount of love, money or ignominious prostration at the feet of our local megatoystore manager made the slightest bit of difference. Nor, strangely, did my threat to expose his nefarious marketing chicanery in an upcoming lecture. Don't these functionaries realize the damage that can be done to a company's reputation when a pompous academic addresses a group of inattentive undergraduates? Capitalism trembles when it hears the baleful scholarly words, "I've got a bullet point with your name on it, buddy."

The oligarchs of the toy industry may have miscalculated the demand for Hogwarts Castles – actually, they calculated their market*tease* perfectly – but there's no shortage of alternative spin-offs to choose from. There are spin-offs associated with what marketers call the "core product," the HP brand itself; spin-offs associated with the product category, what marketers term the "augmented product"; and spin-offs associated with the "extended product," broader socio-economic and cultural concerns.[1] For the purposes of discussion, we'll call them Core Potter, Augmented Potter and Extended Potter respectively.

CORE POTTER

Core Potter spin-offs are those with Warner Brothers' seal of approval. They sport the distinctive lightning-flash logotype and carry less than subtle reminders that "HARRY POTTER characters, names and related indicia are trademarks of Warner Bros. © 2000." This is legalese for "Big Brothers is watching you."

In October 1999, as part of the Harry Potter movies deal, Warner Brothers acquired the property's worldwide licensing rights, reportedly for the relative pittance of $500,000. Warners, in turn, has recruited a roster of licensees – initially 46, rising to 75 – who manufacture a wide variety of merchandise, collectibles and keepsakes. A rolling programme of product introductions commenced in August 2000, when an edited selection of Harry Potter items apparated in the company's 136 Warner Brothers Studio Stores. A second wave was released during the 2000 Christmas holiday season, and at the same time, Warners' distribution channels were widened to include leading bookstores and toyshops. A third wave, again with wider distribution, hit the shores of consumer society in early 2001, though the perfect product storm arrived eight months later, just as the first movie was surfing toward the multiplexes. Further flotsam and jetsam washes up with each ensuing theatrical release, leading many impecunious parents to wonder when the tide will eventually ebb.

Blockbuster movie franchises, as Shone makes clear, rely on three main streams of revenue: fast food, computer games and ancillary memorabilia.[2] Harry Potter is slightly different in so far as Rowling's side of the Warners deal gives her some control over the merchandise issued under her characters' imprimatur, especially in the United Kingdom. Not one to mess about if people mess about with her creation, she has effectively scotched the fast-food option with the unambiguous statement, "I would do anything to prevent Harry Potter from turning up on fast-food boxes. That would be my worst nightmare."

Hamburgers may be out, but soft drink is permissible. Up to a point. A $150 million sponsorship deal was signed with the Coca-Cola corporation in early 2001, though the product is prevented from appearing in the movies, notwithstanding the fact that the ordinary-world scenes are set in the present, where one might reasonably expect to see kids slugging soft drinks. Coca-Cola cognoscenti note that elves, pixies and goblins appear in the movies, so why not Sprites? But Rowling is adamant.

When it comes to computer games, the Harry Potter franchise has been much more successful. Developed by Electronic Arts, the gaming adaptations of the first three movies earned excellent reviews and performed well in a highly competitive marketplace. More than 20 million copies have been sold to date, which is not to be sniffed at. The general consensus is that a $1 billion franchise is on the cards. Attempts to turn Quidditch into a workable computer game have been rather fraught, admittedly. The rules have had to be altered somewhat, and though EA maintains that Quidditch is an imminent gaming monster on a par with *Grand Theft*

Auto, *The Sims* and *Halo 2*, the computer games community remains to be convinced.

Action figures and the like have also been a money-making machine. Mattel alone has unloaded $150 million worth of Potter paraphernalia, and estimates suggest that the total merchandise market is worth approximately $1 billion. However, as this figure is suspiciously like one of the gee-whiz statistics that Harry's marketing minders are famous for, perhaps we shouldn't swallow it whole. Still, it's unlikely that consumers will be running out of keepsake purchasing opportunities any time soon. As ranges come and go, wax and wane, rise and fall, the total number of items available at any moment is uncertain. The general consensus is that around 400 Potter products are currently nestling in the country's supermarkets, toyshops, e-tailers, category killers, department stores, tat merchants et cetera. The principal categories are:

Apparel including T-shirts, pyjamas, socks, pants, sweat-tops, underwear, umbrellas, wristwatches, sunglasses, charm bracelets, backpacks, baseball caps and Halloween costumes (available in all sizes and emblazoned with your favourite figures, be it Dobby, Dursley or Dementor).

Education supplies ranging from pens, pencils, diaries and day planners to binders, bookends, writing sets and tastefully illustrated wall calendars. Best of all is the troll-shaped glue dispenser, which extrudes the sticky liquid as snot (yes, snot).

Household goods: mugs, clocks, ornaments, pillows, posters, photo albums, address books, bedspreads, beach towels, sleeping bags, banners-cum-tapestries, soup bowls, bath products and bathroom-cabinet requisites like glow-in-the-dark Band-Aids (packets of 25, assorted shapes).

Candy and comestibles stretching all the way from Chocolate Frogs (containing Wizard Cards written by Rowling) via cake-decorating kits and pumpkin-drink mixers (with refill) to Bertie Bott's Beans, an assortment of 20 mild-to-wild flavours (including banana, black cherry, booger, bubblegum, dirt, earwax, grass, lemon drop, sardine, toasted marshmallow and – yummy – vomit).

Toys and games comprising a veritable cornucopia of Harry Potter offerings: Lego Hogwarts Express, Diagon Alley, Gringotts Bank, Knight Bus and – damn you, Lego – Hogwarts Castle; Hasbro trading cards and collectibles, including movie stills, Wizard Chess and stereoscopic slides; Gund stuffed animals such as the Scabbers plush doll, Hedwig plush doll, Fluffy plush doll, Hagrid plush doll and a four-foot-long plush Basilisk; and Mattel action figures like Snape, Malfoy, Flitwick, Lockhart and the three principals as "Wizard Sweet Dolls," which come complete with scented bracelets (not their post-troll-encounter scent, I trust).

Sundries: you name it, we got it – limited-edition sculptures, limited-edition Giclee prints, lenticular journals and lunchboxes, purses, wallets, key-rings, tote bags (available in six different kinds of denim including Sparkle and Timberland), snow globes, kites, medallions, stickers, temporary tattoos, secret boxes, story scopes, wind-up tin toys and what can only be described as postmodern pet rocks (semi-precious stones with engravings of Norbert, Mrs

Norris, the Sorting Hat, the Golden Snitch, You-Know-Who and, inevitably, the Philosopher's Stone itself).

Don't all rush at once.

AUGMENTED POTTER

Although WB-licensed products are the most visible manifestation of the HP spin-off industry, they represent but a small fraction of the total. The entire product category – i.e. books – has been sprinkled with Harry's magic marketing dust. They say a rising fad lifts all shops, and that's definitely the case post-Potter. In Britain, for example, a 24 percent rise in the children's book sector as a whole has been reported. Kid lit's break-out, cross-over potential is increasingly recognized too, especially now that adults are prepared to be seen reading the likes of Philip Pullman and Cornelia Funke.

The money-spinning impact of big-budget product launches has not been lost on the book trade either, and in the aftermath of Harry Potter, bookstores, publishers and other players are endeavouring to raise their marketing game.[3] The aim is to become more like the music business or movie industry. A low-key launch with a couple of glasses of warm white wine is insufficient in today's world of first-day grosses, celebrity-studded premieres, OTT publicity stunts and "pedal to the metal" marketing campaigns.

Books, of course, breed books, and few texts are more fecund than Harry Potter. Rowling's writings have spawned a multitude of companions, handbooks, primers, introductions, abridgements, commentaries, counterblasts and exercises in scholarly exegesis. Where will it all end? Before you know it, they'll be writing books about the Harry Potter brand. Have these people no shame? Or dignity?

Space, sadly, doesn't permit detailed study of the Potter ephemera. However, some salient features of the textual topography can be summarized under that plangent mnemonic beloved by precious marketing types, the 4Ps. In this case, the 4Ps of *pirates, parodies, parasites* and *photocopies*:

Pirate copies of the original Potter books are on open sale in India, Africa, America, Britain, Spain, eastern Europe and elsewhere, as are pirated DVDs, computer games, soundtracks and ancillaries (such as Harry Potter Russian dolls). The pirate palm, nevertheless, must go to the People's Republic of China, which has added three entire volumes to the Potter corpus: *Harry Potter and the Leopard Walk Up to Dragon, Harry Potter and the Golden Turtle* and *Harry Potter and the Crystal Vase*. An extract from the first of these is presented in the text panel. I'm no literary critic, but I reckon Rowling isn't exactly chewing the furniture over her Asian amanuensis's writing ability. JK's agents have been chewing the furniture on her behalf, however. Action was taken against Bashu Publishing House, the perpetrators of the pirate editions, and in a landmark blow against the Chinese counterfeiting trade, Bashu withdrew the titles, formally apologized in *Legal Times* and paid a fine of £1,600. Despite this success, it takes more than a slap on the wrist to defeat bookbiz buccaneers. The pirates simply popped up in Russia, where two further additions to the Potter catalogue promptly apparated. Only to promptly disapparate when a Dutch court ruled that the books breached Rowling's rights.

Parodies enjoy an element of legal protection, and when it comes to protected parodies, Michael Gerber enjoys more elements than a parodic periodic table. His three Barry Trotter books have sold some 600,000 copies worldwide, which is a gnat bite on the hide of Harry Potter but the kind of sales figure that most mid-list authors would die for. The three parodies recount the adventures of Barry Trotter, a licentious celebrity wizard who has his wicked way with ghoulish groupies; Ermine Cringer, a nymphomaniacal witch who knows how to knock up a mean love potion; and the one and only Lon Measly, an airhead pal who suffered a unfortunate Quiddit accident that left him with the mental capacity of a red setter, plus some unseemly canine habits. In the first volume, *Barry Trotter and the Unauthorized Parody*, our hero battles against evil Lord Valumart, a maleficent marketing genius. What's worse, he is quickly reduced to a quivering jelly by two of Fantastic Books' black-hearted, soul-sucking employees, the Marketors. Despite this setback, Barry bravely rescues J. G. Rollins, who is locked in a dungeon by Fantastic and forced to write book after book after book. But he fails to stop a Wagner Brothers movie, *Barry Trotter and the Inevitable Attempt to Cash In*. True to his word, Gerber has since cashed in with *Barry Trotter and the Unnecessary Sequel* and *Barry Trotter and the Dead Horse*. No doubt a movie is in the offing.

Parasites are the single biggest category of the para-Potter literature. They are instantly recognizable by the disclaimers prominently emblazoned on the front cover: "This book is not authorized by J. K. Rowling or Warner Brothers." Or words to that effect. These titles are many and varied, and pitched at diverse audiences. They include George Beahm's *Muggles and Magic*, a compendium of all things Potter; David Colbert's *The Magical Worlds of Harry Potter*, a treasury of the myths, legends and fascinating facts alluded to in Rowling's writings; and Roger Highfield's *The Science of*

Harry Potter, an accessible overview of contemporary scientific thought on issues arising from the enchanted texts (Can broomsticks fly? Is time travel possible? Do Bowtruckles you-know-what in the woods?).[4] As if that weren't enough, at least six unauthorized biographies of J. K. Rowling have been written, including one by Sean Smith that upset the celebrity storyteller. Scholastic has also got into the parasite act, with its Harry Potter Literature Guides, as has JKR herself. In 2001, she published two pseudonymous spin-offs, *Quidditch Through the Ages* and *Fantastic Beasts and Where to Find Them,* which raised £15.7 million for the UK charity Comic Relief.[5] What's more, she plans to write a Potter encyclopaedia when the seven books are put to bed and her hero is laid to rest.

Photocopies refer to the burgeoning number of books that are broadly similar to Harry Potter. They involve magic, enchantment, fantasy worlds, adolescent escapades and the eternal battle between good and evil. Photocopies is perhaps too strong an expression for this aspect of augmentation – parallel, pastiche or palimpsest would do just as well – since there is no suggestion of plagiarism or foul play. Nevertheless, they are books that feed the market for Harry Potter-style stories and are often marketed as such ("something to read while you're waiting," "if you like Harry Potter, you'll love this," etc.). Eoin Colfer is perhaps the most obvious example. His Artemis Fowl series hit the bookstores in Harry's post-*Goblet* hiatus, and he took advantage of the market opportunity. Philip Pullman also benefited from Potter's pump-priming, though the *His Dark Materials* trilogy began before Harry hysteria took hold. Michelle Paver

(*Wolf Brother*), Jonathan Stroud (*The Amulet of Samarkand*), Cornelia Funke (*Inkheart*), Graham Taylor (*Shadowmancer*) and Susanna Clarke (*Jonathan Strange & Mr Norrell*) are just some of those following in the footsteps of the boy who delivered big bucks to the book business.[6] I'm sure there's more to come.

EXTENDED POTTER

If the neophyte sorcerer's impact were confined to the book trade or HP brand extensions, it would still be pretty impressive. But the spin-offs extend far beyond the quotidian concerns of those with a paw or two in the Potter pie. The influence of the teenage thaumaturge is felt far and wide. The nation's economic base has been boosted by the boy-wizard bubble. The necromancers on Wall Street and elsewhere have spirited the share prices of Bloomsbury, Scholastic and memorabilia makers like Hornby Trains to extraordinary heights.[7] The global printing industry has received a substantial shot in the arm (and every other appendage, near enough). The road haulage business is stretched to its outer limits during new-title delivery frenzy. The cinemas are packed to the projection boxes, much to the delight of screen advertising agencies who are making the most of their medium during a tough time for the sector. The British acting profession is coining it and benefiting from the international exposure that Hollywood blockbusters bestow, as are film crews, special-effects providers and, not least, Leavesden Studios. The locations used in the movies are proving popular with tourists, though some sites have been chastised by Warners' legal guardians for advertising the connection. That hasn't stopped British Tours from organizing Harry Potter packages that take in Durham Cathedral, Goathland station and Oxford's Bodleian Library, or prevented the British Tourist Authority encouraging visitors to "Potter Around Britain" and supplying maps to assist the happy wanderers. So enthusiastic is the BTA that its US freephone number is 1-866-4HEDWIG.

And there's more. Boarding schools in Britain and France report significant increases in applications. National Health–style glasses are enjoying a Potter-led revival. Opticians claim that kids with perfect eyesight insist on being fitted with magi-frames. Recruitment officers maintain that HP lookalikes are more likely to get jobs than the less physiognomically blessed. EFL teachers report that the texts are ideal workbooks for those wishing to improve their grasp of English, as do parents of children with learning difficulties. Owls are proving increasingly popular as household pets, much to the dismay of animal rights activists, who have triggered a to-whit to-do about owners' inability to care for the often irascible creatures. As if that weren't enough, Britain's bookmakers offer odds on everything from the movies' box-office performance to the likely survival of crucial characters. However, when a £20,000 punt was placed in Liverpool a few days after a truckload of pre-publication copies of *Phoenix* was hijacked, the bookmaker wisely decided not to accept the bet on Sirius Black.

To cap it all, an international trading incident was almost caused in early 1999 after American aficionados started snapping up copies of *Chamber of Secrets* from Amazon's UK website several months prior to its intended American release. Scholastic claimed that the practice violated its territorial rights, Amazon responded by restricting sales to one copy per order, and the US edition was published four months ahead of schedule. The problem recurred later the same year when the UK edition of *Azkaban* appeared in July 1999 and Scholastic rushed it into print two months later. The editions have been published simultaneously ever since.[8]

While it is an exaggeration to state that when our cub sorcerer sneezes the economy catches cold, there's no denying the market power of the Harry Potter effect. Harrymania, however, isn't just about money. He's more than a mere figure, albeit an impressive figure, on the economy's bottom line. To the contrary, the trials and tribulations of the spellbinding schoolboy have escaped the economic base and colonized the cultural superstructure. The Potter parlance of "Muggles," "Quidditch," "Slytherin" and so on has not only entered everyday discourse, but is treasured by its users (surveys show that "Quidditch" is Britain's second favourite word, after "serendipity"). The name Harry is back in fashion, as the annual rankings of the most common boys' names make clear (up from thirtieth in 1994 to sixth in 2000). Edinburgh's recent designation as the world's first City of Literature is at least partly attributable to the reputation of its bestselling citizen (who wrote the preface to Auld Reekie's application). Sermons predicated on the wonderful wizard of Hogwarts are preached from pulpits around the country. Cartoons, situation comedies, soap operas, talk shows, radio round-tables, after-dinner speeches and syndicated newspaper columns routinely refer to Rowling's remarkable creation – he was parodied on *SNL* and in *Mad* magazine, for example – as do many of her cultural peers. Harry is mentioned in Dan Brown's blockbuster *The Da Vinci Code* and is the subject of a game of charades in Pixar's *Monsters Inc.*, though the intertextual laurel surely goes to Dawn French and Jennifer Saunders' spoof movie, *Harry Potter and the Chamberpot of Azerbaijan*.

And that's not all. Rowling has appeared on the cover of *Time*, *Newsweek* and the *New York Review of Books*, among many others, and is one of the few Britons to have featured in *The Simpsons*. Her fictional familiar, meanwhile, has captured the front cover of *Vanity Fair*, *The Face*, *Heat*, the *Sunday Times* magazine, the *Financial Times* magazine, *Premiere*, *Empire*, *Entertainment Weekly* and – whoa! – *Marketing Business*, to say nothing of the Christmas double issue of *Radio Times*. Indeed, in an astonishing acknowledgement of Rowling's cultural achievements, BBC Radio 4 cleared its schedule on Boxing Day 2000 to broadcast an eight-hour uninterrupted reading of the first novel. The Bible, as one cynic observed at the time, is abridged for Radio 4. Harry's holy writ, however, mustn't be tampered with.

In addition to bedazzling the BBC, Harry Potter has been held responsible for some weird and wonderful happenings. These include the election victory of Holland's prime minister, Jan Peter Balkenende, who looks a bit like the boy wonder; the architectural imaginings of the Prince of Wales, who has built a meditation space in Highgrove based on

Hagrid's hut; the plight of postal workers, whose health and safety is adversely affected by carrying bulky Harry Potter parcels during new-title saturnalia; the physical and mental damage done to children who suffer from aliments like Potter elbow, caused by the sheer weight of the post-*Azkaban* volumes, or Harry headache, due to reading too quickly during marathon all-night sessions; the staggering fact that whereas only 8 percent of the UK population can spell Jane Austen's name correctly, 85 percent are spot on with Hogwarts; [9] and, get this, the anger of a disgruntled politician who objected to the depiction of Dobby the house-elf in *Chamber of Secrets* since it was obviously based on him. His name? Vladimir Putin.

Although there is no shortage of contenders, perhaps the strangest HP spin-off of all is that sales of (real) broomsticks have taken off, manufacturers of (authentic) magic wands can't keep up with the demand, and enrolments in (bona fide) schools of witchcraft and wizardry are on the up and up.

Actually, stranger still are the HP ecstasy tablets (featuring a screen shot of Daniel Radcliffe) currently on sale in New York's clubland, and the Harry Potter therapies offered by self-help, empower-yourself, get-in-touch-with-your-inner-hippogriff gurus on the wacky west coast of the United States.

Well, OK, strangest of all is the unanticipated use that one of Mattel's toys is being put to, allegedly.[10] A vibrating broomstick that makes whooshing, swooping and analogous erogenous noises, Mattel's Nimbus 2000 has been selling like hot cakes in the kind of retail outlet where Aunt Petunia fears to tread.

Hey, who needs a Nimbus when Vernon's on hand?

The Critics Story

Hath not the potter power over the clay, of the same lump to make one vessel unto honour, and another unto dishonour?

Romans 9: 21

FREE LIFT INSIDE

There's a curious astromarketing phenomenon studied by generations of skywatchers and salespersons, called a "total eclipse of the market." Its periodicity is as yet unknown, but its mechanics are well understood. A marketing event occurs and such is its commercial candlepower that every other contemporaneous marketing occurrence is overshadowed and cast into darkness.

Harry Potter is one such phenomenon. Every time a Harry Potter is released, the remainder of the book market is eclipsed. Even the remainders. I know this from personal experience because I once had a book published in Potter's penumbra. It was called *Free Gift Inside!!*, and even though it contained a chapter on the boy wizard (in a pathetic, parasitic attempt to cash in), it was quickly consigned to the textual knackers' yard, along with its luckless predecessors.

About nine months after *Free Gift Inside!!* flickered and died, a book called *Free Prize Inside* was published. Written by Seth Godin, the guru of viral marketing, it was not unlike my own humble effort. The cover design was based on a broadly similar breakfast-cereal theme; the mini case-studies overlapped somewhat; and the basic anti-orthodoxy message of his book was akin to my own. Naturally, my first thought was that the sod had ripped me off and, in my caffeine-fuelled paranoia, I rapidly worked out the ways, means and methods of the rapscallion's actions. The fact that his book promptly soared to the upper reaches of the bestseller lists had nothing whatsoever to do with my righteous writerly rage. Honest.

After ruminating on writs and other nonsense, as one does, I came to my senses and accepted that these things happen, coincidences occur and, as Jung informs us, synchronicity exists.[1] His book was much better than mine, what's more, and, let's be honest, I was hardly in a position to complain since I myself had been trying to benefit from the Harry Potter spill-over.

And I'm not the only one. As we have seen, lots of people have attempted to sneak on board the Hogwarts gravy train, without so much as a by-your-leave, let alone a ticket (see text panel on p. 116). Even the critics of the boy wizard benefit by association, inasmuch as their criticisms are publicized only on account of the Potter connection. The critics of the critics attract attention on the same basis, as do the critics of the critics of the critics, as do the critics of the critics of the critics of the critics . . . and so on *ad infinitum*.

Harry Potter, in short, exudes the "oxygen of publicity," and there's no shortage of heavy breathers. The critics, if truth be told, are almost as plentiful as Harry Potter tie-in merchandise. But rather less attractively packaged. As with the action figures, they come in many ranges and sizes, each with a different pose or function to perform. Some even have lenticular articulation, whatever that is, while most have xtra-long-life batteries included. Broadly speaking, four main categories of critique can be identified: the *literary*, the *learned*, the *righteous* and the *rest*.

GOBLET OF IRE

The principal problem exercising literary critics is the artistic merit of Rowling's books. Are they classics or not? Are they

FAKING HELL

Free lifts are one thing, fraudulent fakes are quite another. In 2001, an astonishing story broke about the Harry Potter brand. According to Nancy Stouffer, a little-known American children's author, she had written some books back in the early 1980s featuring creatures called "muggles". Stouffer also claimed to have penned a picture book featuring a character called Larry Potter, who wore glasses, possessed wayward black hair and had a friend called Lilly. Granted, there were some significant differences between Stouffer's creations and Rowling's – her muggles were hairless creatures with elongated ears and big bellies – but the parallels were sufficiently close to give the reading public pause. Or so she alleged.

J. K. Rowling, understandably, was taken aback by the accusations. "It was as if some strange woman had come out of nowhere saying she was my children's mother," she subsequently observed. Although JKR has never downplayed her influences, or denied her sources of inspiration (Harry Potter got his name from a childhood acquaintance), Nancy Stouffer was most definitely not among them. Rowling's legal team filed suit; Stouffer filed counter-suit; and, after the case wound its way through the American legal system, Judge Allen G. Schwartz ruled that Stouffer's claims were not only baseless but fraudulent. The typographical fonts used in her books, for instance, weren't available until the 1990s, and invoices that purported to prove her books' circulation figures were shown to be invalid. In addition to having her unfounded allegations dismissed, Stouffer was fined $50,000 for fraud and ordered to pay Rowling's costs. When Stouffer appealed the decision in December 2003, what's more, the Second Circuit affirmed Judge Schwartz's original decision in its entirety. Although Stouffer's "muggles" undeniably predated Rowling's, the court found that "the similarities between Stouffer's books and the Harry Potter series are minimal and superficial."

Dismissed though it was, the Stouffer case reminds us that storytelling can damage as well as enhance. Even false stories circulated about Rowling are absorbed into the meta-story and can tarnish her good name long after they've been proved groundless.

worthy of the attention they've received? Do they do anything that hasn't been done many times before? Do they deserve a place in the kid-lit pantheon alongside Lewis Carroll's Alice books, C. S. Lewis's Narnia series, Kenneth Grahame's *Wind in the Willows* and Mark Twain's *Huckleberry Finn*? The answer, it seems, is a resounding no.

According to Anthony Holden, a leading light of the British literary establishment, Harry Potter represents a triumph of puffery over poesy.[2] Bloomsbury, he claims, consistently resorts to hype worthy of Wonderbra. J. K. Rowling, he bellows, can't write to save her life, is afflicted with a "pedestrian, ungrammatical prose style," generates less dramatic tension than an average soap-opera episode, and churns out cloyingly sentimental storylines that are clichéd, unimaginative and all too predictable. What's more, she is personally responsible for the infantilization of British culture and owes much of her success to Bloomsbury's perfidious marketing department, with its disingenuous spin-doctors, devious strategic planners and not-so-hidden persuaders. Naturally, he goes on, neither personal animosity nor – heaven forbid – professional jealousy plays any part in his attack on Harry Potter. On the contrary, he wishes the royalties-replete author well, whilst urging her (in a sadly clichéd, unimaginative and all too predictable expression) to take the money and run.

Not to be outdone, the prominent US literary critic Harold Bloom has poured scorn on the horror that is Harry Potter from the *Wall Street Journal's* magisterial pages.[3] So upset was the bookish behemoth – Harold Bloom is the Giant Haystacks of American letters – that he excreted a recommended reading list of his own, *Stories and Poems for Extremely Intelligent Children of All Ages*. He also affably informed Harry Potter's 35 million US readers that they didn't know shit lit from shinola and, on the basis of a quick perusal of the first Potter novel, concluded that Rowling's prose style is "heavy on cliché, makes no demands upon her readers" and will eventually find its place among the "vast concourse of inadequate works" that cram the trashcans of the ages.

Equally affronted is the memorably monikered children's literature authority Jack Zipes.[4] The Harry Potter phenomenon, he trumpets, is completely inexplicable in kid-lit terms. The books are formulaic and predictable. "If you've read one," he notes formulaically, "you've read them all." And there is, he goes on predictably, "nothing exceptional about Rowling's writing in comparison with that of many other gifted writers of children's and young adult literature." The only way of accounting for the Potter Ponzi scheme, Zipes concludes, is that it's an iniquitous capitalist conspiracy. It's a money-making monster that tempts young readers into its mephitic, memorabilia-baited lair, leaving little or nothing for more worthy children's authors. One fears he's been reading too many fairy stories.

More recently, A. S. Byatt, the Booker Prize–winning author of *Possession*, set about the teenage mage in the *New York Times*.[5] Whereas great fantasy writers like Tolkien, Terry Pratchett and Susan Cooper are capable of inventing secondary worlds, Rowling's is at best a "secondary secondary world": unoriginal, hackneyed and cobbled together from the jolly-hockeysticks school story and *Star Wars*. Harry Potter, she announces, is "written for people whose imaginative lives are confined to TV cartoons and the exaggerated (more exciting, not threatening) mirror-worlds of soaps, reality TV and celebrity gossip." No envy there, then.

The foregoing are just some of the many literati who have taken a swing at J. K. Rowling.[6] The critical twitterings of intellectuals, however, are as nothing compared to the condescension of awards juries and bestseller-list compilers. In late 2000, J. K. Rowling was denied the Whitbread Book of the Year when the award was given to Seamus Heaney for his translation of *Beowolf*, another tale of magic and mayhem. Earlier that year, the *Sunday Times* controversially excluded Harry Potter from its prestigious bestseller list, apparently on account of the books' disreputable kid-lit provenance.

More astonishing still, the world's foremost arbiter of literary endeavour reconfigured its bestseller list in the wake of the boy wonder's dominance. Beset by complaints that the Potter-led list was preventing the appearance of old-line literati like John Updike, Philip Roth and Saul Bellow, the *New York Times* took decisive action.[7] On 23 June 2000, when the publication of *Goblet* would've given Rowling four of the list's top five places, she disappeared from it completely, only to reappear on a special children's bestsellers list. Not long after, the children's list was further subdivided into paperback, picture and chapter lists, one of which is published each week. Although some see this decision as a continuation of intellectuals' long-standing prejudice against children's literature, it can also be considered a remarkable testament to Rowling's impact. As even Harold Bloom was forced to admit, "she has changed the policy of the policy-maker."[8]

PEDANT PENDANTS

To be sure, the Bloom with a view doesn't simply bestride American letters; he looms large in academia too, though he is something of a litcrit misfit. His professorial brethren, nevertheless, have descended on Harry Potter like a plague of literary locusts. Dissertations, masters' theses, PhDs and learned, all-too-learned articles are pouring out of the scholarly sweatshops as I write. Symposia, colloquia, workshops and conferences are spreading like kudzu grass among the sylvan groves of academe. A dedicated academic database lists approximately 500 publications on the Potter phenomenon thus far.[9] That's more than enough to be getting along with, you might think, but the pedantic production line is only warming up. As the years go by and as HP is institutionalized through courses, modules, textbooks, readers, teaching aids and the rest of the pedagogic apparatus, the professionalization of Potter will accelerate. Although it may be a while before the He Who Must Not Be Named professorial chair is established at Bob Jones University, it won't be long, surely, before the Rubeus Hagrid Chair is endowed at Harvard, Oxford or Exeter. Harold Bloom, presumably, is entitled to first refusal.

When the corpus of Potterania is examined – I've read them so you don't have to – it's clear that the incumbents of the ivied ivory tower are exercised by three main issues. The first of these is the antecedents of Rowling's creation. Roald Dahl's *Matilda*, Enid Blyton's Malory Towers series, Thomas Hughes' *Tom Brown's Schooldays*, Anthony Buckeridge's *Jennings Goes to*

School, Jill Murphy's *The Worst Witch*, Ursula Le Guin's *A Wizard of Earthsea*, T. H. White's *The Sword in the Stone*, Diana Wynne Jones's *Charmed Life*, Eva Ibbotson's *The Secret of Platform 13*, Ed Stratemeyer's Hardy Boys, Frank Richards' blessed Billy Bunter books and, Gurg help us, Franz Kafka's "In the Penal Colony" are just some of the many sources that Rowling is channelling. And then, of course, there's the continual comparisons with C. S. Lewis, Lewis Carroll, J. M. Barrie, L. Frank Baum, J. R. R. Tolkien and all the rest.

The second scholarly matter is Harry Potter's positioning on the spectrum of political correctness. Regrettably, he doesn't do too well. Rowling has been lambasted for her failings on the feminist front. According to Christine Schoefer and others, the books lack strong female figures, are irredeemably patriarchal in tone, endorse narcissistic recourse to the depredations of cosmetic surgery (most notably Hermione's orthodontic enhancement) and take recidivist pleasure in phallocentric wand waving.[10] Sometimes, as Freud almost said, a wand is just a wand, but not for radical feminist academicians, it seems. Politically, too, the texts are traduced by the house-elf sub-plot, which only serves to reinforce the subordination of subaltern species. The lamentable acronym SPEW is indicative of Rowling's irredentist inability to take serious issues seriously, notwithstanding her laudable attempts to raise classist, ageist, racist and muggleist matters in a work of fiction. She's not very nice about fat bastards, either.

The third topic is explanatory. Why has Harry Potter taken off the way he has? What are the reasons for the books' unprecedented success? This issue, suffice it to say, has exercised many great minds and spawned all manner of hypotheses. These range from the most obvious (they're great stories, well written) to the most obscure (it's all down to memetics). Somewhere in between lie the mathematical (power law probability distributions), the memorial (it's due to nostalgia, today's preoccupation with yesteryear), the malevolent (a heinous media cabal's behind Harry), the mischievous (sheer good fortune), the marketing (a schoolyard buzz-based brand) and the postmodern melding of demographic cohorts (kidults, tweenagers, age compression, etc.) As I explain in more detail on my website, however, none of these explanations holds water, not even the much-vaunted buzz-marketing scenario.[11] The only thing scholars are sure of is that they're unsure about the causes of our Potteraceous Age.

ST BRUTUS SAVES

For all their critical caterwauling, academicians are fairly harmless. They truly believe that their words of wisdom will change the world, though as their words are largely incomprehensible that ambition is a tad ambitious. They also work on the premise that close reading and textual exegesis will bring multinational capital to its knees. Slapping its thighs, I reckon. Still, they're nice to have around. They work for peanuts and keep an eye on the kids for a couple of years.

The kids are also on the minds of the righteous, a much more influential critical mass than the ivory tower internees. They stoutly maintain that Rowling's books are corrupt and corrupting. They are not afraid to say so and even less afraid to take up arms against a sea of thestrals, or anyone else who deems Harry harmless. For those who subscribe to the Word of the Lord, the Potter books are an abomination, despite Rowling's protestations that her tales have a deeply moral core and are celebrations of friendship, loyalty and the ongoing battle of good against evil.[12] And despite the benefits that flow from the books, such as opening children's eyes to the pleasures of reading, the Saved see only the cloven hoofprints of Satan. They note with particular dismay the oft-recycled story of Rowling's "apparition," when a fully formed Harry Potter suddenly appeared to the author while she was sitting on a train from Manchester to London. For biblically minded Baptists, this is as close to a diabolic Damascene conversion as is (in)humanly possible.

Although the anti-Harry attacks of shadowy southern pressure groups such as PAPPY (Pilgrims Against Potter's Profanities, Y'all) are perhaps the most influential wing of the righteous right, they aren't the only one. Alongside those who worry about Rowling's promulgation of paganism or regard the stories as signposts on the road to hellfire and damnation, there are those who object to unChristian acts contained in the books (lying, cheating, betrayal, rule breaking, authority usurpation, underage drinking and so forth), those who consider them much too scary for young children (as does Rowling herself), and those who are disturbed by the deaths that are mounting up volume by volume, each one more traumatic and terrifying than the last (though compared to many computer games nowadays, HP's body count is negligible).

Accordingly, the Potter books have been banned, burnt, boycotted and belittled by bellicose Bible-thumpers. In Australia, sixty schools run by Seventh-day Adventists exorcised the texts, as did the Christian Outreach College in Queensland. In Poland, the Catholic church campaigned against the books' use in a national literacy campaign. In Germany, leading theologians have warned about the books' baleful influence on young minds. In Austria, a Harry Potter hate line was set up for those who wished to ring and record their parental disapproval. In the United Kingdom, schoolteachers' unions have expressed concern about the stories' ability to make the occult attractive, and St Mary's Church of England School in Chatham, Kent, has censored Rowling outright. Similar actions have been taken in Canada, UAE, Taiwan and, not least, the United States. The American Library Association reports that Harry Potter topped the "most challenged" book list for several years in succession. By 2000, the books had been challenged (i.e. complained about formally) in 25 school districts in at least 17 states, including California, Oregon and Colorado, as well as the Bible-belted and -braced southern heartlands. At least two book-burning incidents have been recorded, one in Penn Township, Pennsylvania, the other in Alomogordo, New Mexico.

AS GOOD AS ARREST

Christian fundamentalists are one thing, Wicca chicks are quite another. A New Age sect in southern California has complained about Rowling's misrepresentation of the craft, arguing that the belligerence in the books does no favours to the thaumaturgic lifestyle, which is based on peace loving, tree hugging, skinny dipping and suchlike. Indeed, it sometimes seems that everyone is a critic when it comes to Harry Potter.

To pluck a few examples at random: Jonathan Meades, an opinionated architectural pundit, argues that "They are absolute shit, just terrible, worse than Enid Blyton. I have discouraged my children from reading them...It's like they're written by a focus group. J. K. Rowling is the sub-literary analogue of Tony Blair."[13] Felicity Kendal, a thespian fondly remembered for the 1970s sitcom *The Good Life*, contends that while Rowling has done much to encourage reading among today's MTV generation, her books hardly qualify as classics. "A classic," she opines, "is more than a smash hit; it has to have something to do with inspiration and a great deal more to do with some inexplicable magic that places one word before another to create a rhythm and form that defies analysis."[14]

Even Stephen King, who knows more than a modicum about writing smash hits and is often pigeonholed alongside Rowling as a leading light of lowbrow literature, is occasionally catty about his youthful rival. True, he has published several adulatory reviews, most notably in the *New York Times (Goblet)* and *Entertainment Weekly (Phoenix)*. In the former, however, he condescendingly notes that the Potter books provide an excellent grounding for young readers who'll eventually graduate to the classics, such as those written by his good self. In the latter, the Gilderoy Lockhart of schlock horror criticizes Rowling's prolixity, particularly her adverbial excesses. Being accused of prolixity by Stephen "crank 'em out" King is surely the ultimate insult. With friends like that, who needs Jonathan Meades?

When it comes to carping, moreover, the books are just the beginning of it. Almost every aspect of Potterity has been taken to task at one time or another. The beneficial effect of HP on the reading public – encouraging kids to abandon Playstations et al. – has been called into question, as has the purported post-Potter increase in public library usage. The movies have received a pasting from the professionals, largely because of their extreme fidelity to the books and consequent lack of dramatic tension. Indeed, *Rolling Stone* refused to review *Chamber*, which it considered second-rate franchise fodder, and reviewed the five-star movie marketing campaign instead.

Not everyone, however, is enamoured with the marketing. In fact, if there is such a thing as a consensus position on Harry Potter, it is that the books and movies are unremarkable (if successful) but the merchandising is unforgivable. Harry Potter, many critics believe, is a marketing scam from start to finish. The success of the series is due to hype, spin, hoopla and similar PR stunts. So meretricious is the marketing, apparently, that concerned journalists periodically publish damning critiques of Harry-hawking. It has been estimated – shock, horror – that it takes £400 to kit a kid out with the full Potter regalia. The price of the toys (rip-off), the failings of the manufacturers (batteries not included), the inadequacies of the assembly instructions (I couldn't put it together) and the sheer amount of stuff (where will it end?) are lambasted from the hallowed columns of our nation's great organs (unbesmirched as they are by crass commercial considerations). As two aghast *Sunday Times* journalists observe:

> Children can wake up on Harry Potter sheets, brush their teeth with his toothpaste, wash their hair with his shampoo, take their Harry Potter rucksack to school, use their Hedwig, Bertie Botts and Gryffindor notebooks in class, drink their Harry Potter colas, eat from themed lunch boxes, check the end of the school day on their Harry Potter watches and go home to play on electronic games starring the boy hero before doing their homework on Harry Potter desk sets and curling up again in bed in pyjamas emblazoned with his image to reread the novels using a Harry Potter bookmark.[15]

Faced with such damning evidence, many might surmise that a massive imposture is being perpetrated on the consuming public by heartless marketing types. Alternatively, one could conclude that attacking cheap 'n' nasty Harry Potter tie-ins has become a Fleet Street Christmas tradition, alongside reviews of the year, platitudinous op-eds about world peace, office party etiquette guides and lists of perfectly awful gifts for people who give perfectly awful gifts to you. On slow news days there's nothing like a Harry Potter rip-off story to get the readers riled up and persuade Outraged of Tunbridge Wells to dip his pen in vitriol. It sells a few extra papers as well.

REMEMBER THE ALOMOGORDO

As a marketer, I can't help being amused by the huffing and puffing of Harry's critics. The contention that Potter's popularity is a consequence of marketer manipulation indicates that they overestimate the extent of marketing's ability to bewitch. Try, try, try as marketers might, they can't sell crap. Well, not complete crap anyway. Harry Potter may be crap, as certain self-important scholars suggest, but it's crap that strikes a chord with innumerable consumers. Harry Potter doesn't have to be sold. He sells himself. Marketers aren't to blame. Nor can they take the credit.

Another aspect of Pottermarketing that many critics misconstrue concerns the wealth of merchandise that's available. Far from being unspeakably ubiquitous, Harry Potter has been merchandised comparatively carefully.[16] Only 75 product licences have been issued, compared to the hundreds that could have been signed. Approximately 400 items are available, which seems like a lot – and indeed is – but it's small beer when set against broadly similar cultural brands such as *Jurassic Park* or *The Phantom Menace* or *Batman*. Granted, there have been more complaints about the HP tie-ins, which may be attributable to the powerful emotional attachment that many people feel toward the novels (they haven't had time to bed in or cool down culturally the way that *Batman* or *Star Wars* have). But the fact of the matter is that the Potter memorabilia business is nowhere near as bad as it could have been.

In addition to this misunderstanding of merchandising, there's the small matter of selling books. The critics of Harry hoopla often act as if the boy wizard has written the book on book marketing, as if we're witnessing the kind of shilling that's never been experienced before, as if we've entered a whole new dispensation of marketer manipulation. Again, this is not so. Thirty years ago, *The Country Diary of an Edwardian Lady* was spawning tie-ins like there's no tomorrow. Sixty years ago, the Tarzan books by Edgar Rice Burroughs came with a raft of jungle collectibles, gee-gaws and loincloths, to say nothing of numerous movie adaptations. A hundred years ago, L. Frank Baum's *Wizard of Oz* triggered a national craze for Woggle-Bugs, a toy based on one of the storybook characters.[17] Baum, moreover, adapted his own series for the stage, formed a production company to make one-reel movies of his literary creations and, several decades before Walt Disney's Magic Kingdom, seriously considered setting up an Oz theme park on the Californian island of Catalina. His irreligious books were banned, burnt and boycotted for good measure, even after the 1939 movie was canonized as an American classic. There's nothing new under the marketing sun, especially not in the book business.

Above and beyond the critics' bibliographic myopia, there's a final marketing curiosity, the most curious curiosity of all: namely, critics' unwitting complicity with Harry Potter's marketers. As every brand wrangler knows, there's nothing like a little criticism to fan the marketing flames. Apart, of course, from a lot of criticism. Critique, censure and controversy are the 3Cs of effective marketing communications in our mass-mediated world. This is especially the case with cultural product categories like books, movies and music, where the number of near-identical competing products is enormous. Controversy has an inbuilt buzz factor that attracts affronted onlookers and gets them talking or, better yet, arguing about Eminem's latest video nasty, Matthew Bourne's *Swan Lake*, racy TV series like *Desperate Housewives*, grisly video games such as *JFK Reloaded*, or whatever it happens to be.

Controversy, it has to be stressed, isn't a cast-iron guarantee of success – things can go badly wrong, as Janet Jackson's studied wardrobe malfunction bears witness – but when it's done properly, a kind of countervailing critique is called forth.[18] Every attack by the anti-Potter contingent precipitates a counterattack by pro-Potter patriots. For every Harold Bloom there is an Alison Lurie. For every Anthony Holden there is a Bel Littlejohn parody. For every A. S. Byatt there are bloggers who deem her comments a goblet of bile. For every Jack Zipes or Christine Schoefer there are hundreds and hundreds of Harry Potter fanatics who give off to the gurus on radio phone-in programmes. For every PAPPY, furthermore, there is a PADDY (Pagans Against Dumbledore-Dissing Yellowbellies). For every Nancy Stouffer there are Pottermaniacs who think nothing of making death threats against, or taking pot shots at, uppity authors who accuse J. K. Rowling of plagiarism. Stouffer should think herself lucky they didn't use the Cruciatus Curse.

Crucio Godin!

9

The Consumers Story

You are really cool! You are my hero!
You kicked Voldemort's butt! You rock!

Fan letter to Harry Potter

THE WORK OF ART IN AN AGE OF HARRY POTTERMANIA

Just before the Second World War, the German cultural critic Walter Benjamin wrote an insightful essay on the ancient art of storytelling. This art, he argued, owed much to the interventions of merchants and traders, who not only circulated stories throughout the prehistoric world but also employed their sales-pitch prowess to improve the telling of the tales. They knew from their day-to-day commercial experiences how to hold an audience, how to overcome its disbelief, and how to close the sale-cum-tale.

Walter Benjamin's essay wasn't a celebration, however. On the contrary, he maintained that the ancient art of storytelling was in terminal decline. The modern world of mass production, mass consumption and mass communication was undermining humankind's ability to weave compelling tales:

> Less and less frequently do we encounter people with the ability to tell a tale properly. More and more often there is embarrassment all around when the wish to hear a story is expressed. It is as if something that seemed inalienable to us, the securest among our possessions, were taken from us.[1]

The great essayist was writing in 1936, at a time when freedoms were being curtailed throughout Germany and the fate of Jewish intellectuals was uncertain. He died trying to escape less than four years later. His pessimism, therefore, is understandable. Still, if ever a cultural critic got it wrong, it is surely Walter Benjamin. Seventy years on from his learned lament, storytelling is stronger than ever. Stories occupy our every waking hour – in newspapers and magazines, on television and radio, over tea or coffee, down the pub, at the water cooler, surfing the net, in movies, plays, songs and books – and, if dreams are included, our sleeping hours as well. Stories, as literary critic Kenneth Burke observes, are equipment for living.[2]

FANON AND ON AND ON

If stories are equipment for living, then Harry Potter consumers are fully loaded and having the time of their lives. Perhaps the fullest expression of people's preoccupation with the wizarding world comes in the form of fan fictions. These are *entire* HP novels, near enough, written by fans using Rowling's characters and posted on dedicated websites. According to fanfiction.net, the foremost clearing-house for this kind of thing, approximately 64,000 additions to the Harry Potter corpus currently exist. The same website, by contrast, lists 600 additions to the *Artemis Fowl* series, some 350 contributions to *His Dark Materials*, less than 200 addenda to Stephen King's ample oeuvre (most of which he probably wrote himself) and 7 extrapolations of Dan Brown's *Da Vinci Code*. Even *Star Trek* and *Lord of the Rings*, with 3,000 and 14,000 offerings respectively, don't come close to the lord of the ring-binders.

In addition to this so-called "fanon" – most of it pretty innocuous, though some is downright pornographic[3] – Harry Potter's fan base exhibits its enthusiasm in several less

YOU KNOW YOU'RE TOO BIG A FAN WHEN...

- You mutter Latin nonsense words under your breath.
- You call your least favourite teacher Snape.
- Your computer says "You've Got Mail" and you run outside looking for an owl.
- Your sort everyone you meet into the four Hogwarts houses (Gryffindor, Ravenclaw, Hufflepuff and Slytherin).
- You had to go to hospital when you broke your nose running head first into the wall between platforms 9 and 10 at King's Cross.
- You collect plugs.
- Before getting up to fetch something, you always try to summon it first. *Accio TV remote!*
- You spend hours tapping bricks in special orders hoping that a secret entrance to Diagon Alley will appear.
- When playing chess, you yell orders to the chess players and get upset when they don't move.
- You get emotional every time you hear "Hedwig's Theme."
- You say "wicked" all the time because Rupert Grint does.
- You name all your pets after HP characters.
- You know that Harry's birthday is 31 July 1980, Hermione's is 19 September 1980 and Ron's is 1 March 1980, even though the books never said.
- You went out and bought the latest edition of Webster's Dictionary because they added the word "muggle."
- You were kicked out of the cinema for standing on your chair, throwing your shoe at the screen and yelling "That didn't happen in the book!"

Source: mugglenet.com/funlists/

asinine ways (see text panel). Hundreds of tribute web sites exist, such as mugglenet.com, hpana.com and hp-lexicon.org, that serve different segments of the icon's consumer constituency. The amount of Potter art out there is legion, including lots with Harry and Draco in compromising positions (don't ask). Not to be outdone, amateur video-makers are having a field day with the boy wonder, spoofs of imagined movie trailers being especially popular. As if that weren't enough, every titbit of Harry Potter trivia is webcast to the digitudes who respond instantly with postings, parsings and opinions. When A. S. Byatt threw her hissy fit in the *New York Times,* a tornado of antagonistic commentary tore through cyberspace, flattening every gimcrack chat room in its path.

And then, of course, there's eBay. When it comes to the biggest bring and buy sale on the planet, Harryheads are among the biggest bringers and buyers around. On any given day, thousands of Potter products are in play: everything from *Philosopher's Stone* movie posters signed by the entire cast (a snip at £770) to quasi-decapitated Hermione dolls that have seen better days (either that or she's doing a Nearly Headless Nick impersonation). It is impossible even to guesstimate the size of this market, though I suspect that the number of transactions exceeds the total for brand-new merchandise, in volume if not in value.

More important, this activity indicates that consumers of the Harry Potter brand aren't content to remain at the receiving end of marketing strategies. They are marketers themselves. They sell as well as buy. They are part and parcel of the Potter business. They take great interest in the performance of the brand – box-office takings, computer-game sales, share price of Scholastic et al. – and in marketplace gossip generally. When the HP brand was ranked fourth on *Forbes'* fictional characters' list, website notice boards were inundated with boosterish, successories-style statements from aspiring CEOs among the fan base. "Way to go, Jo." "We'll be number 1 next year." "Come on HP!"

POTTER PATTER

The consumers of the Harry Potter brand, then, are anything but passive. Hyperactive doesn't begin to describe it. Forget fluoride, the sooner Ritalin is put in the water supply, the better for all of us. Especially Warner Brothers.

Warners, it's fair to say, has found it difficult to come to terms with HP's e-empowered customers. As the music business discovered with illegal downloads and as the movie business is rapidly finding out, today's iGeneration consumers make it very difficult for companies to hold the copyright line. Attempts to do so are met with ridicule, hostility and reams of unwanted publicity, which only perpetuates the activity it is supposed to curtail.

Thus, when Warners acquired the Potter property, it sought to shut down the unofficial websites that were proliferating at the time. Unfortunately, it tangled with Claire Field, a 15-year-old Harry Potter enthusiast who was so smitten that she'd constructed a cyber shrine to him and his chums.[4] Warners' precipitate attempts to close down her site were widely publicized and even more widely condemned. The company ended up looking like a heavy from one of its own 1930s B-movies – come back Jimmy Cagney, all is forgiven – and diverse Defence Against the Dark Arts websites sprang to her aid. A boycott of tie-in merchandise was briefly mooted before Warners sensibly withdrew its writ and settled the matter amicably.

The situation with fanfic is even more awkward, since Warner Brothers has very strong grounds for taking legal action on account of consumers' disfigurement of its property. But the act of doing so merely inflames the fan fiction community, who are thereby given a priceless opportunity to pose as battlers against big business, right-on radicals sticking it to The Man. From a consumer activist standpoint, it doesn't get any better, short of being incarcerated without food or water.

It seems that the hydra of cyberspace can't be beaten by conventional means, much less by weapons of mass litigation. Wisely, therefore, Warners now works with its fanbase, as do the other stakeholders in Brand Harry Potter. Nowadays, the WB, Bloomsbury, Scholastic and Rowling websites go out of their way to encourage consumer participation. Site visitors are variously sorted into houses, signed up for classes, given Quidditch try-outs, allowed to earn house points, encouraged to solve puzzles and invited to submit stories, express opinions or recount uplifting Potterbrand experiences. They are also given an opportunity to add to their painstakingly assembled portfolio of HP investments. The soft sell, in short, has replaced the hard fist of cease and desist.

While management consultants might argue that the companies concerned are making insufficient use of their cyberdistribution channels – sell more, faster! – this low-key approach is eminently sensible. Numerous studies of fan communities show that although they are suckers for stuff, they hate being sold to.[5] They like to think of themselves as discerning connoisseurs cast adrift in an ocean of dross, not hopelessly brand-obsessed saps who'll buy anything companies chuck in their direction. It's unwise to disabuse them.

SLOUCHING TOWARDS BETTELHEIM

To be sure, only a fraction of Harry Potter merchandise is sold or swapped or salivated over on-line. The bookstores, movie houses, toyshops, hypermarkets, video-rental outlets, computer-games emporia and second-hand retailers aren't exactly short of real-life customers either. Back in 2001, when consumers were understandably reluctant to splash out in the aftermath of 9/11, Harry was anointed by the RL retailing community as the boy who saved Christmas. Halloween is becoming something of a Potterfest too: a time when consumers' expensively acquired wands, robes, broomsticks and glow-in-the-dark glasses can be shown off to all and sundry. Can "Trick or Trelawney" be far away?

Several Harry Potter collectors' conventions have also been held, usually in conjunction with conferences and colloquia, such as Nimbus 2003 in Orlando, Nimbus 2005 in Salem and Accio 2005 in Reading. The august environs of Sotheby's and Christie's are similarly echoing to the sound of eager Potter bidders. The rare-books market in particular has been revolutionized by rampaging Harry hordes, much to the astonishment of old-school collectors. First editions of *Philosopher's Stone* are especially prized, largely on account of the limited print run and the fact that many were bought by libraries, which means pristine copies sell at a premium. A high-quality copy can fetch £20,000-plus at auction. In late 2002, a signed copy sold for £23,800. A set of four "associational" copies owned by and inscribed to Rowling's father commanded $87,6000 at a Sotheby's sale in December 2003. What's more, a single sheet of paper containing the author's 200-word abstract of *Phoenix* went for £28,260 at a charity auction in 2002. The cover art for the books has broken sales records as well. Thomas Taylor's original watercolour for *Philosopher's Stone* sent dealers into a tizzy when it fetched £85,750 in July 2001. A year later, Peter Wright's *Chamber of Secrets* original failed to reach its £30,000 reserve and was withdrawn from sale.

Needless to say, there is much debate among bibliobibuli, as H. L. Mencken famously described them, about this Potter-fuelled inflationary spiral. Most think it won't last and many refuse to handle Rowling editions at all. As the celebrity rare-book dealer Rick Gekoski notes in his analysis of the HP brouhaha, "I have seen them catalogued for as much as £25,000. For that price, for God's sake, you could buy a pretty good *collection* of W. B. Yeats, or Conrad, or D. H. Lawrence." Mind you, W. B. Yeats's corpus never spawned ceramic keepsakes of Wild Swans at Coole, or action figures of dancing dancers, let alone Lego construction kits of Thoor Ballylee. One suspects that the old till fumbler would've trousered his share of the take with alacrity.[6]

TRADE SOFTLY BECAUSE YOU TRADE ON MY DREAMS

For all the RL action, there's no denying that the serried ranks of cyberconsumers are inordinately attractive to market researchers. Ease of access, geographical reach and the sheer loquaciousness of the on-line community are almost irresistible to individuals engaged in consumer research. Netnography, a kind of on-line in-dwelling, is the consumer research technique of the moment.

Rebecca Borah, for example, has surfed the highways and buyways of the worldwide web, conversing with Potterphiles, Weasleymanes and Grangerphagites.[7] From her analysis of message-board postings, she calculates that two-thirds of Potter posters are under the age of 18, with most falling between 12 and 16. Of the 12 to 16 subgroup, approximately two-thirds are female, though male participation is much greater in movie-related message boards. Borah followed up with email interviews of twenty teenage consumers and found that most had been introduced to Harry by a friend or relative, many had participated in school activities pertaining to Potter, around half had made objects inspired by the books, such as wands, artwork or costumes, and the majority were keen to acquire official Warner Brothers merchandise. However, her interviewees are by no means Pottermonogamous, since

Pokémon cards, favourite TV characters and pop-band fandom also figured prominently in the discussions. Far from being brand loyal, teenage consumers are quite profligate with their preferences. Harry Potter may be the crack cocaine of kiddie culture, but he is still only one among many brand-name intoxicants.

Fascinating though her findings are, Borah's research predates the deluge of movie tie-in merchandise, as well as the creative hiatus between books 4 and 5. It fails to give a complete picture, furthermore. The problem with studies of Harry Potter fan communities, or any self-selected enthusiasts, is that they are utterly atypical. As only the most obsessive Potterites are prepared to write *entire novels* about his ongoing adventures, or produce mini-movies, or build tribute websites, or pay £700-plus for an item of memorabilia, their views hardly reflect those of the average Potter punter. They aren't even typical of HP admirers, most of whom are less committed to the cause, and they certainly aren't typical of the population as a whole, which remains largely unmoved by the escapades of Hagrid, Hedwig, Hermione and the rest. True, opinion polls show that approximately 60 percent of America's teenage population are favourably disposed toward Harry Potter, with 25 percent of adults feeling likewise.[8] Yet impressive as this is – especially for a character in a book – it's important to keep things in perspective. The first-day DVD sales of, say, *Spiderman* comfortably exceeded the first-day sales of the fifth book. Most consumers are Potterphobes, not Potterphiles. Or Potter impartials, at least.

BROWNIAN MOTION

In order better to understand the range of consumer responses to Harry Potter, I've been conducting a rolling programme of qualitative research among young adults.[9] This research programme employs a storytelling methodology that I've developed down the years and used to study brand images, TV advertising campaigns, retail store atmospherics, individual magazine ads and shopping behaviour generally. Space doesn't permit a detailed presentation of my findings, or even a defence of the methodology, which yields more insights, I maintain, than traditional qualitative research techniques like focus groups and depth interviews. Nevertheless, a brief overview of the preliminary results may prove useful.

As might be expected, just about everyone has *heard* of Harry Potter and has some familiarity with the Harry Potter phenomenon. Let's be honest, the guy's impossible to avoid, though that hasn't stopped people trying. The idolization of Harry Potter, interestingly enough, is very off-putting for many consumers. His popularity with some makes him unpopular with others. They are determined to resist his bewitching blandishments at all costs. They pride themselves on not being taken in:

> The crazy over-the-top media frenzy surrounding the whole phenomenon acts as a barrier preventing me from taking the bold step of reading a Harry Potter book or watching any of the films... Even if I was to sit down and watch one of the movies any enjoyment would be tarnished by the continual feeling that this is a box-office hit, adored by millions and a regular feature in the

Sun newspaper... I think I have this attitude simply because I'm generally a person who doesn't like to conform with popular opinion. It's more fun to be different.

(David B.)

They also hate Harry Potter devotees, with their knowing smiles, secret language and embarrassing enthusiasm:

It's just gone Halloween and the number of fake Harry Potters and Hermiones I saw on a night out was crazy. Big fat women trying to fool themselves that they look good dressed as Hermione when all they look like is a man in drag, bad drag at that! I don't know who they are trying to kid but the only guys that seemed to be attracted to them were Harry Potter wannabes. Where did all these people come from? All these people who think dressing up as school kids is a turn-on! Surely this is verging on perversion.

(Kim P.)

These perceived barriers to entry, furthermore, are reinforced by incessant peer pressure. Everyone knows someone who suffers from Pottermania – a parent, a cousin, a friend – and the goddamn maniac is determined to spread the good word, which further alienates the agnostics. While one hesitates to call this bullying, it's a lot closer to Dudley Dursley than J. K. Rowling and co. might imagine:

I like to think that I have managed to remain neutral about Harry Potter, but because I am not a devout fan this can be very testing. It's a bit like Christianity. Harry Potter lovers feel that they must spread the message of the "good book." They automatically make a dash for non-believers with the aim of saving them from their non-Harry Potter ways.

(Gemma A.)

Being browbeaten into reading Harry Potter isn't the only point of entry, it must be emphasized. My findings show that people get sucked into Potter's parallel universe in a number of different ways. The idea that consumers follow a preordained HP progression – what economists term path dependency – which starts with the books, continues with the movies and culminates with the merchandise is completely at odds with reality. Some are drawn in by the films, others by watching the videos, others by catching a trailer, others by encounters with the tie-ins (being asked to buy a present for someone), others by a family connection (reading bedtime stories to a nephew), others by gifts or prizes or sales promotions (free tickets to the premiere courtesy of Coca-Cola), others by the phenomenon itself (what's all the fuss about?) and yet others by default (there's nothing else to read). Harry Potter is a brand smorgasbord. People pick and mix. Some pile their plates high, others are content to nibble. Many suck it and see.

When people *do* fall for Harry Potter, however, they fall big. They have the zeal of the newly converted. They refuse to let minor inconveniences, like being on honeymoon, get in the way of their obsession:

In April this year, my girlfriend had just become my wife and we were about to set off on honeymoon. We had an hour or two to kill in Gatwick and I did some last-minute panic buying for some holiday reading... I decided to buy the first two Harry Potter books, the *Philosopher's Stone* and the *Chamber of Secrets*. I have got to say I was something of a Harry Potter virgin, that is to say I had never read anything by J. K. Rowling, hadn't seen the films or knowingly bought any affiliated wands or broomsticks. I was however only too aware of the publicity surrounding the books and who the author was, as well as some of the characters... When I got down to reading, I felt the books were brilliant. I could really see how the books appealed to adults and children alike. Needless to say that my new page-turning obsession did not go down too well with my new life partner. When on our first night in the Maldives and expecting some form of conjugal rites, she found herself in second place to a fictional 11-year-old trainee wizard and something called the Sorting Hat.

(Keith T.)

Even those who hate Harry Potter with a vengeance find that their temper is tempered when they are required to read the books or watch the movies. They may not like the boy wizard – and like his admirers even less – but at least they understand why the fans feel the way they do:

Watching the film provided me with a glimpse of why so many older people worship Harry Potter. On one hand it may be the idea that takes them back to their childhood days. I can relate to this theory. On the other hand it may be that it takes them away from the mundane reality of their own lives. As you get older it gets increasingly harder to have fun. Worries about the mortgage, worries about the kids, worries about the kids having kids, and so on. So for those few brief moments I realized that perhaps it wasn't just a stupid childish fad, it had a real offering for the older generation too.

(Richard H.)

Now, this doesn't mean that once consumers take a hit of Hogwarts they are hopelessly addicted and thereafter hang on Rowling's every word. On the contrary, most consumers are self-conscious about their fixation – especially those who have been Pottermanes from day one – and are actually quite relieved to discover that there are people much more obsessed than them. I'm sad, as it were, but not *that* sad!

Other enthusiasts adopt a kind of wry detachment from the whole thing. Yes, they love the books. Yes, they rush out and see the movies. Yes, they buy the DVDs and other bits and pieces. But let's not get carried away. It's only a bit of fun, after all:

> I've become a Harry Potter junkie. I need my fixes to keep me spellbound. Aaarrrggghhh!!! There are a few things that annoy me though – the names of the characters, a lot of them end in "us" or similar, such as Cornelius, Albus, Lucius, Sirius (seriously now, come on), Serverus (cut me some slack), Bartimus (Simpsonus) and so on... There's another thing that annoys me, the not naming of people and things, it's like *The Village,* the "you-know-what" and "those-we-don't-speak-of" and "the-place-we-don't-go." Crap, crap, crap. Name them – Voldemort – it is a bit hard to say and I admit it took ME several times to get it right. But now I'm a wizard at it.
>
> (Daria C.)

Some customers, similarly, appropriate the product and take it to places that Warner Brothers never anticipated:

> All the Harry Potter novels have provided many a laugh for me but some have spilled over into my social life. After a crowd of my mates and I went to watch the first movie, it is not uncommon for the following phrase to be shouted out randomly on a night out. "You're a wizard, Harry!" may seem a bit strange to onlookers, but believe me it is bound to have us in stitches. And of course it is a lot funnier when you are drunk!
>
> (Kim P.)

Many consumers, in short, are quite proprietorial about Harry Potter. They feel a very strong sense of ownership.

Personal friendship, near enough. As such, they are contemptuously dismissive about certain parts of the movie adaptations:

> The saying goes that the books are much better than the films and in my view this is certainly true. I can't believe [*Chamber of Secrets*] left out the hilarious picture of the Weasleys degnoming their garden. The film does not match the vivid and detailed descriptions that I have conjured up when reading the book. I imagine Gilderoy Lockhart with long blond flowing locks that he is constantly flicking back. As orange as Dale Winton and just as camp. The book leads me to think he is much more pompous and exaggerated than in the film. The film was a great let-down of the character I had built up.   *(Gemma A.)*

Not even the books are exempt. Quite a few feel *Phoenix* wasn't up to the previous high standard (a view, incidentally, shared by lots in the fanfiction community, who aren't reluctant to excise it from the canon), and worry whether Rowling will be able to do justice to the neophyte magus now that the series is reaching its climax and the whole world is wild about Harry:

> The build-up to the fifth book was immense, it was the longest book but in my opinion very disappointing... How could this woman who has written four such wonderful books ruin it all with her latest release? I was looking forward to continuing the Harry Potter experience but for me the fifth book ruined it... I just hope that the sixth book proves me wrong. Could Rowling really start to go downhill? Did she reach her peak? I hope not.   *(Susan Mc.)*

Ex-enthusiasts, furthermore, feel that the phenomenon is rapidly running out of steam, that it has become too popular for its own good, that it is being milked dry and merchandised to death. Thus, when Rowling announces that another character's about to die – yawn – the news is interpreted not as an intriguing HP tease but as a sign that the series is on the skids. Sensationalist sales tactics are a cry for help, don't you know:

> When I was driving into town the other week the news came on and hey, guess what? Yes, that's right, one of the articles of news was about how J. K. Rowling had stated that she was going to kill off a character in her new book. This got me thinking. My initial reaction was not one of excitement or who will it be, but a very negative "this is just a publicity stunt." I thought "Is Harry slowly dying and was this just a clever PR stunt to help revive Harry Potter?" I think so. I suppose if I was a true Harry Potter fan (which I can assure you I never will be) I would be ecstatic. But I think this is because I have watched as the media and companies drown Harry Potter out and have made me sick to the back teeth of Harry Potter... I simply do not give a gryffindor about Harry Potter in my everyday life. My life is too busy to care about Harry Potter and what J. K. Rowling wants to do next. I simply have no interest. *(Laura O'K.)*

Harry isn't history yet. But he's heading that way.[10]

10

The Brands Story

There is a misconception that identity and branding are primarily about uniformity: they need to be about uniformity only when the nature of the organisation demands it. Perhaps the organisation with the most uniform identity in the world is North Korea. How many brands want to emulate North Korea?

John Simmons

HARRY POTTER AND THE TESCO COMESTIBLE

It was my wife's birthday the other week, and hopeless romantic that I am, I bought her a birthday cake in Tesco. A Harry Potter birthday cake. A Prisoner of Azkaban birthday cake. Not that I'm implying she's a Dementor or anything. Truth to tell, I bought the cake because of Harry Potter's striking image, which was carved in multicoloured icing on top of Tesco's calorie-crammed indulgence. The striking thing about it was that, well, Harry had obviously put on quite a bit of weight while no one was looking. For a second I thought I'd picked up Harry Porker by mistake. But no, it was the boy wonder astride his trusty Firebolt, ostensibly in the middle of a game of Quidditch. And boy, did he have a middle, though it was his face where the additional poundage really showed.

Needless to say, Harry's alarming avoirdupois caused much consternation in our Potter-preoccupied household, and not a little speculation on the possible causes of his condition. One faction surmised that it was simply post-pubescent puppy fat, which will doubtless be shed in the fullness of time. Wrestling with Voldemort must burn up the calories, right? Another faction, of a less forgiving bent, inferred that all those multi-course meals with extra helpings at Hogwarts – coupled with copious Chocolate Frogs, Bertie Bott's Beans and similar sugary snacks – were finally taking their toll on the increasingly troll-like teenager.

Yet others focused on Potter's porcine physiognomy and hypothesized that calorific overload had nothing to do with it. He was either on steroids to enhance his athletic performance, or had been hit in the gob by an especially errant Bludger. Is there a plastic surgeon in the house? Or a drug tester? I mean, is the Firebolt capable of carrying such loads? Where are the health and safety people when you need them?

Regardless of the reasons for Potter's roly-poly state, his cake contributed to our family's celebratory mood and provided a moment or two of innocent fun. It wasn't the tastiest birthday cake we've ever eaten, but it's certainly the most talked-about. In this respect, Tesco's Azkaban comestible conveys an important lesson about products in general and brands in particular. There's much more to a brand than the physical product or service itself. Brands offer more than use value, or functionality, or performance, or utility. They are symbols, signals, indicators, talking points. They are objects of display, contemplation, conversation or envy. They are repositories of meaning. Cakes contain more than two layers of sponge with jam filling and icing on top, important though core ingredients are to consumers' overall experience. They contain nourishing narratives as well.

WHAT'S IN A NAME?

Marketers, admittedly, have long been aware that there's more to brands than product attributes and user benefits. Brands carry all sorts of subtle and not-so-subtle connotations.

An Armani suit says something about its wearer, as does an Audi A4, a bottle of Asahi, an Aldi carrier bag. Brandsperanto is our universal language, Malltalk our vernacular.

When it comes to managing meaning, moreover, marketers have long been urged to appropriate part of the linguistic spectrum and make it their own.[1] That is, to commandeer a word, an idea, an image, a phrase that they can build their brand upon. Virgin is fun. Coca-Cola is it. McDonald's is family. Budweiser is true. Danone is health. BMW is performance. Calvin Klein is sex. Absolut is art. Evian is purity. Avis is effort. Guinness is fortitude. Marlboro is freedom. Nordstrom is service. Polo is discernment. Volvo is safety. Oxfam is relief. Starbucks is respite. Intel is inside. Microsoft is megalomania. The list is endless. Even endless, thanks to Energiser, has been appropriated by energetic adjectival appropriators.

What we're witnessing, I suppose, is the lexical equivalent of the Oklahoma Land Rush, where the Oxford English Dictionary is being overrun, staked out and turned into paying marketing propositions. The process originally dates from the late 1950s, when Rosser Reeves developed the idea of the Unique Selling Proposition and relentlessly hammered it home, a bit like his legendary Anacin adverts. It was reinforced in the 1970s, when Al Ries and Jack Trout positioned themselves as the gurus of positioning, a kind of perceptual pallisading process whereby brands occupy a clearly identified place in consumer cognition. Indeed, the notion is still going strong, though it now trades under terms like brand identity, essence, DNA, spirit, promise, personality, mission, vision, value, soul and mindshare. A recent book by Matt Haig studied 100 leading brands, each one of which was allocated a piece of terminological real estate: Nokia, the streamlined brand; Colgate, the total brand; Google, the search brand; Xerox, the research brand; Kleenex, the disposable brand, and so on.[2]

The basic problem with this semantic strip-mining is not that the dictionary has been exhausted by corporate colliers. With twenty volumes and counting, the OED reserves are more than sufficient for marketing's foreseeable demands. The problem is that the very idea of one word one brand is untenable in today's incurably ambiguous world. Assumptions of stable linguistic meaning have foundered on the shoals of post-structuralism.[3] Chaos theory, the tipping point and those fluttering butterflies in the Amazonian rain forest that cause hurricanes in Hong Kong constantly remind us of the hair-trigger character of our unstable times. The old idea of the unified self or personality has been superseded by a mutable post-modern sense of self where people possess a multiplicity of personae that they adopt as occasions demand – wife and mother, career woman, sports fanatic, fashion victim, culture vulture and so on. In such vacillating circumstances, it is little wonder that the word "brand" is used in at least fifteen different ways, though this figure is but a fraction of the fluctuating total.[4]

Once again, marketers are well aware of this issue. There is increasing evidence to suggest that we're moving away from the epoch of monolithic marketing – monosyllabic marketing, if you will – to a polymorphic marketing dispensation. Ambi-brands are all around, as are pluri-appeals and multi-strategies. Southwestern Airlines offers outstanding customer service *and* rock-bottom prices. Target, a much-admired American houseware outlet, retails exclusive products to a mass market. The Gap built its reputation on cross-generational appeal. Reebok makes sportswear for couch potatoes. Starbucks sells the ultimate commodity in an ultra-commodious manner. Red Bull astutely combines hedonism and health, energy and enervation, the injurious and the innocuous. Donald Trump disburses advice on getting rich while his casinos languish in Chapter 11. Madonna adopts and abandons every image imaginable, from sexually ambiguous virago to Kaballah-espousing supermom. The old strategic matrix of Michael Porter – *either* cost *or* differentiation *or* focus – has imploded. Contemporary brands are happy to combine cost and differentiation (and throw in focus for fun). Stuck in the middle, or completely outside the box, is the place to be nowadays.

PARADESSENCE PLEASE

The ambiguity at the heart of twenty-first-century brand culture is aptly captured in the novel mentioned earlier, Alex Shakar's *The Savage Girl*. Set in the cool-hunting department of a trendy research company, Tomorrow Inc., it posits that "paradessence" is the key to successful brand building. Paradessence, according to Chas Lacoutere, the CEO of Tomorrow Inc., invariably involves an irresolvable paradox. Products blessed with paradessence combine two mutually exclusive states and satisfy both simultaneously. Ice-cream melds eroticism and innocence. Air travel offers sanitized adventure. Amusement parks provide terror and reassurance. Cars render drivers reckless and safe. Sneakers grasp the earth and help consumers soar free. Muzak is a hybrid of transience and eternity:

> 'What's the paradessence of coffee?' Chas asks her.
>
> *Paradessence?* She came across the word *essence* in a couple of the marketing books she skimmed, usually attached to some glib distillation of the product's selling points. But *paradessence?* What could that mean? Something paradiselike, perhaps.
>
> She takes a shot. 'I guess something about how it wakes you up, maybe. Or the way it warms you up on a cold morning.'
>
> 'Waking and warming,' Chas says. 'Very close. Now think. Locate the magic. Locate the impossibility.'
>
> 'The impossibility? I don't know. Being warm. That's kind of like being sleepy, I guess.'
>
> 'The paradessence of coffee is stimulation and relaxation. Every successful ad campaign for coffee will promise both of those mutually exclusive states.' Chas snaps his fingers in front of her face. 'That's what consumer motivation is about, Ursula. Every product has this paradoxical essence. Two opposing desires that it can promise to satisfy simultaneously. The job of the marketer is to cultivate this schismatic core, this broken soul, at the center of every product'.
>
> *(The Savage Girl, pp. 72–3)*

The paradessence of Harry Potter is magic and mundanity. The books treat magic as an everyday technology – a commodity, in fact – that can be learned or acquired and used for eminently practical ends. Argus Filch's Kwikspell correspondence course epitomizes this naturalized supernaturalism, as does the magical merchandise on sale in Diagon Alley and Hogsmeade, as do Gilderoy Lockhart's battalion of self-help how-to rough-guide bestsellers, as do the no-nonsense classes at Hogwarts in everything from potions to transfiguration. As Marina Warner adroitly points out, "the students at Hogwarts only have to learn spells, like lessons, or acquire the right brand of weapon, to become lords of creation themselves...This is commodity magic, the enchanted realm of the logo."[5] It brings to mind Arthur C. Clarke's much-quoted quip that "any sufficiently advanced technology is indistinguishable from magic."

This melding of technology and magic isn't the only ambiguity in HP. The judicious combination of literary genres, the mixture of past and present, the appeal to parent and child alike, the ambivalent treatment of good and evil – which shows that just as there is evil in good (Harry isn't perfect, nor is his father, and he's affiliated to Voldemort), so too there's good in evil (Snape isn't all bad, Sirius Black's not a mass murderer, there's more to the dreadful Dursleys than meets the eye) – are just some of the undecidables in Rowling's brilliantly bewitching ambibooks.

The critical reaction to the novels is no less contradictory. As we have seen, some consider them a collection of clichés; others feel they're wonderfully written. For every critic who disses the books as hackneyed and derivative, another deems them delightful and hilarious. Numerous commentators regard them as monuments to marketing hype, yet equally many see Harry

Potter as a fan-led phenomenon. For the Harold Blooms of this world, they are transparent and obvious tripe. For the Stephen Frys, they are delightfully cryptic and deliciously equivocal. To read them out loud is "like swimming in chocolate," he declares.

This latter-day rise of ambiguous brands isn't a cause for concern. Contradiction, inconsistency, uncertainty and discord are very much in keeping with our tumultuous times. Nor does it mean that meaning doesn't matter. It means that meaning is more multi-faceted than before. As Wally Olins notes, "Many great brands are like amoebae or plasticine. They can be shaped, twisted and turned in all sorts of ways yet still remain recognizable."[6]

Nor, for that matter, is this a matter of aspiring to ambiguity. Ambiguity isn't right for every brand or every occasion. In circumstances where there is a clear-cut choice between competing products, as in the most recent US presidential election, there's much to be said for consistent, insistent, unwavering appeal. Flip-flop marketing is punished at the point of sale. But not every choice is so sharply defined. Very few are, in truth, especially when there are countless nearly identical products to choose from, as is increasingly the case in twenty-first-century consumer society.

At the risk, then, of being unequivocal when equivocation is called for, it is evident that the old principles of branding, where an individual brand stands for one thing and one thing only, are being superseded by the idea that branding is an ambiguous business.

Ambiguity is not easy to sell, however. "Ambi-brand" isn't the kind of neologism that'll barnstorm boardrooms worldwide. The remainder bins perhaps. A better CEO-trap is called for. A metaphor possibly.

FANTASTIC BRANDS AND WHERE TO FIND THEM

Take rainbows. To my knowledge, no one in the consultancy–industrial complex has ever championed the idea of rainbow brands. Yet rainbows are an extraordinary natural phenomenon, one that has captivated humankind since the dawn of time.[7] From Anaximenes and Aristotle to Descartes and Newton, great minds have struggled to explain the luminous arc of triumph that appears intermittently, beguilingly, evanescently. Artists and poets, moreover, have often attempted to evoke the heart-stopping ravishment of encountering rainbows in the raw, the wild, the free, in all their multi-hued glory.

Such is their primal power, indeed, that myths about rainbows abound. There's a pot of gold at its scintillating end. It's a bejewelled bridge between God and man. It's an omen of impending doom. It's a symbol of peace and reconciliation. Pointing at rainbows is bad luck. If you pass underneath a rainbow you'll change sex. Alchemical rainbows materialize when base metal is transmuted into gold. The Greek goddess of rainbows, Iris, transmits Olympian messages to mere mortals (somewhat akin to Hermes, the trickster god of the marketplace).

It seems to me that great brands are like rainbows. They are marvellous. They are mysterious. They are radiant. They captivate, enrapture, dazzle. They stop us in our tracks. In a world of adjectival inflation, where awesome means great, excellent is good and terrific bespeaks indifference, rainbows remind us of what awesome really means. They are awe-some. Gucci. Rolex. Lamborghini. Takashimaya. *The Simpsons.* Harry Potter's Firebolt.

Like rainbows, great brands are rare. They are few and far between. They emerge fully formed, often when least expected (Barbie, Tiger Woods, Greenpeace). Not every brand can be a great brand – though that shouldn't prevent us trying – and not every great brand remains one (British Airways, David Beckham, the Conservative Party). Yet no matter how cluttered the brandscape gets, there's always room for another rainbow brand. They are a sight for sore eyes.

Like rainbows, great brands don't outstay their welcome. Nothing is more guaranteed to denude a brand's appeal than ubiquity. When ubiquity strikes, obloquy isn't far behind, and obituary's a real possibility. Something that's seen constantly isn't seen at all. Less is always more, provided the moments of more-ness are spectacular, stunning, sublime: glimpsing a Ferrari F430, gasping at Olympic opening ceremonies; delighting in children's excitement during HP book-release frenzy.

Like rainbows, great brands are wonderful, inasmuch as they induce a sense of wonder among consumers. Your first encounter with a great brand is an unforgettable experience. Tiffany. Selfridges. Guinness. The Guggenheim, Bilbao. It is love at first sight and, although that initial moment of *ravissement* can never be repeated, it never leaves you either. *Pace* Wordsworth, "My heart leaps up when I behold/A rainbow brand array."

Like rainbows, great brands are unique. Scientists tell us that everyone sees rainbows differently; it all depends on where the observer stands in relation to the sun and light-bending raindrops. Although rainbows are similar in overall form, they are in fact highly individual. The same is true of great brands. They look the same. One Ford T-Bird or Louis Vuitton suitcase is very much like another. But they mean different things to each owner, consumer and admirer. They are bespoke and bespoken.

Like rainbows, great brands are colourful. Unlike the beige uniformity of everyday life and every other brand – neutral, nondescript, mediocre, magnolia – rainbows inject a much-needed burst of technicolour that uplifts, energizes and makes the world a better place to be, if only momentarily. Indeed, just as the number of colours in the rainbow has been debated for centuries – Aristotle says three, Newton says seven, today's best guess is infinity – so too rainbow brands generate discussion, controversy, argument. Is Bose better than Bang & Olufsen? Does Malmaison match Soho House? Galliano or Gaultier?

Like rainbows, great brands are all image. They are optical illusions, tricks of the light. They don't exist, except in the eye of the beholder. Analogously, great brands are inherently intangible. Their greatness lies in that certain something – call it *je ne sais quoi* – that competitors conspicuously lack.

As everyone knows, the top brands in any given category are pretty much of a muchness in terms of technology, performance, service, bells-and-whistles. They have to be, otherwise they wouldn't be among the top brands. Great brands, however, offer something extra, something special, something impalpable. They are extra-ordinary. Literally. They provide what also-ran brands provide and something extra as well. Truly great brands, what's more, have an unerring ability to extract the extra, exploit the extra and extend the extra into other seemingly unrelated categories: Amazon, BMW, Caterpillar, Dunhill, Nike, EasyJet. OK, scrub EasyJet.

Like rainbows, great brands aren't customer-led. They appear when it suits them. They don't emerge to order. They are what they are. They invite us to participate, partake, experience, enjoy. But they won't do as they're told. Take them or leave them. It's well known that consumers don't know what they want and great brands know that consumers don't know. Not that this means that great brands like Harvard, Harley or Hooters are anti-customer. Far from it. It simply means that they aren't customer-centric, let alone driven by focus groups. If anything, they are concept-centric: true to the ethos, the world view, the underpinning belief system of the brand.

Like rainbows, great brands are a puzzle. They are inexplicable, enigmatic, mysterious. They reveal their secrets slowly. There is always something more to discover, an additional nuance or snippet of brand lore that adds to the attraction, appeals to aficionados and reinforces

BRAND RIP, BRAND MIX, BRAND BURN

Nowhere is the rainbow bridge better illustrated than in the case of Apple. Apple is arguably the greatest great brand. It is the cult brand of cult brands. It remains something of a rarity, with a fairly small market share. Ubiquity would be the death of Apple. It evokes a sense of customer wonder, as the rapturous reception of the iPod testifies. It is inimitably unique, a genuine one-off.

When it comes to colourful, Steve Jobs is the dream-coated Joseph of Silicon Valley. As images go, moreover, Apple is image in excelsis (cf. the momentous *1984* TV ad). It is a perpetual puzzle, inasmuch as the brand perplexes and infuriates its followers in equal measure. Important though he or she is, the customer doesn't come first at Apple. The brand is essentially idea- and innovation-led.

Above all, perhaps, Apple is a reservoir of much-retold stories, tales, anecdotes, myths and legends. It lurches from triumph (Apple II, Mac) to disaster (Apple III, Newton) to triumph (iMac, PowerBook, iTunes) and no doubt will continue to do so (risky retail stores?)

Not only is Apple the ultimate rainbow brand, as the logo bears brilliant witness, but it found the pot of magic marketing gold at the rainbow's glided end. When all is said and done, Apple is the brand that lived.

customers' conviction that they've made the right choice, that they are one of the elite, the discerning, the chosen few. It is no accident that many rainbow brands inspire incredible consumer devotion – cult-like followings, in fact: *Star Trek*, ESPN, BlackBerry, Beanie Babies, eBay, Diesel, Ikea, Apple (see text panel). The frequency with which rainbows feature in religious iconography should also give us pause.

HARRY POTTER AND THE SEVEN SEMINAL STORIES

Like rainbows, furthermore, great brands are storehouses of stories. They attract tales and taletellers, as Cyan's "Great brand" series attests. Everyone has a great brand story to tell – a Nordstrom story, a JetBlue story, a Saab story, an Apple story, whatever – and, more important, it's a story that they *wish* to tell. The seven colours of the rainbow parallel the seven basic plots that allegedly underpin the western narrative tradition, brand narratives included. These plots range from bright red (romance) to deepest purple (epic), via blue (tragedy) and green (comedy). The best stories are those that weave different parts of the narrative rainbow together. According to Christopher Booker, Harry Potter melds five of the seven archetypal plots, though the two that Rowling omits (tragedy and rebirth) may yet come to pass.[8] Great brands too have their triumphs and disasters, peaks and troughs, rags and riches. Rainbows require both rainfall and sunshine. So it is with great brands.

Harry Potter provides proof. In *Goblet of Fire*, the book's magical marketing moment – the Quidditch World Cup Final – is prefaced by the following truly awesome occurrence on behalf of brand Ireland:

> Next moment, what seemed to be a great green and gold comet had come zooming into the stadium. It did one circuit of the stadium, then split into two smaller comets, each hurtling towards the goalposts. A rainbow arced suddenly across the pitch,

connecting the two balls of light. The crowd 'oooohed' and 'aaaaahed', as though at a firework display. Now the rainbow faded and the balls of light reunited and merged; they had formed a great shimmering shamrock, which rose up into the sky and began to soar over the stands.

(Goblet of Fire, pp. 94–5)

Hail Harry Potter!

11

The Concluding Story

Business books are written by
evangelical illiterates to convert
the ambitiously gullible.

Jonathan Meades

THE HARRY POTTER WAY TO
HIGHER PROFITS

As I'm sure you know, there is an unavoidable problem with
"way to" books. They suffer from the *In Search of Excellence*
effect, otherwise known as the Tom Peters jinx. That is to say,
as soon as brands, products or organizations are written about
by well-meaning management consultants, they lose their
way and head straight for insolvency city. Alleged examples of
this Ebola-like influence include Gary Hamel's *Leading the
Revolution*, which lionized Enron, that much-admired
paragon of CSR; Jim Collins' gazillion-selling *Good to Great*,
which championed Circuit City as a low-key corporate
role model only to see the company's fortunes plunge
precipitously; and Stephen Brown's less-than-gazillion-selling
Free Gift Inside!!, which sang the praises of Boeing's celebrity
CEO, Phil Condit, just as he fell from grace and his company
slipped into a tailspin.[1]

In such circumstances, I'm understandably hesitant to
extract general lessons from the Harry Potter brand, especially in
chapter 11 of this book. However, I'm going to tempt fate anyway.
The first lesson is that marketers have much to learn from the
books business in general, and kid lit in particular. Far from
being Wussville-on-Wye, as many engine-block and ball-bearing
manufacturers imagine, the book business is a paradigm of
today's Entertainment Economy. Although it is one of the oldest
industries around – Caxton was a marketer before marketing
was invented – the bookbiz is a harbinger of how twenty-first-
century business will be. It is fast-changing, fad-prone,

hit-driven, increasingly global and consolidating rapidly. It is facing technological threats, savage competition, copious substitutes, product profusion and channel confusion. Engine-block or ball-bearing making is child's play by comparison.

Children's literature, likewise, is more than a Cinderella subject. As a long line of authorities from Bruno Bettelheim to Philip Pullman note, it deals with the really important issues that lad lit, chick lit and punctuate-properly-or-else lit refuse to address. Issues like death, duty, good, evil, friendship, forbearance, our place in the world and the fate of the planet. Kid lit plumbs the depths of the human psyche and taps the wellsprings of consumer society. We can and should learn from fairy stories.

HARD KNOCKS ALUMNI

The second lesson is that it's not necessary to be trained as a marketer in order to succeed as a marketer. Richard Branson, David Blaine, Damien Hirst, Larry Ellison, Elliott Spitzer, Digby Jones, Tom Ford, Mel Gibson, Alan Sugar, Steve Jobs, Jim Cramer, Madonna and the king of the comb-over himself, Donald Trump, are all extremely astute marketing people, as is J. K. Rowling. Yet none studied marketing in a formal sense. Their lack of exposure to the finer points of PEST, SWOT, 7Ss, five forces, 4Ps, 3Cs, etc. hasn't been a hindrance to them. On the contrary, it's one of the causes of their success. Not the only cause, of course, but one of them. They haven't been contaminated by marketing's increasingly creaky concepts, pensionable principles and mouldering maxims.

Think about it: every year, the world's universities extrude hundreds of thousands of MBAs, specialist masters and doctorates, as well as innumerable business studies graduates, all of whom have been taught to think about marketing in exactly the same way. They study the same textbooks, learn the same acronym-littered language and approach marketing problems from the same analytical angle. They are blinkered in their thinking, and because they are so numerous nowadays, those fortunate few *without* formal marketing training are at a competitive advantage.

This is especially so in the many and varied sectors of the entertainment economy – movies, music, computer games, etc. – where the standard textbook ideas never applied in the first place. They were developed for, and work best in, the world of fast-moving consumer goods, though many of today's expensively educated, B-school–burnished executives are unaware of this. It follows that as MBA-blinkered marketers increasingly penetrate the entertainment economy, opportunities for those who haven't been indoctrinated will become ever more apparent. Unless, of course, marketing radically rethinks its basic premises and takes its cue from the world we live in today. But the possibility of that happening is a fairy tale, worthy of J. K. Rowling at her most imaginative.

MATRIOSHKA MARKETING

Marketers, then, should make a point of studying the marketeasing impresarios of the cultural industries, if only as a source of uncontaminated competitive advantage in our world of Stepford brands. In this regard, Harry Potter reminds us of a third issue that marketers mustn't forget in their rush to develop meaningful marketing metrics, calculate marketing's contribution to the bottom line and generally prove that marketing is as hard-edged as the rest. That is the importance of mystery. Yep, *mystery*.

Marketing is inherently mysterious, and we forget this at our peril. It is mysterious not only in the sense that we still don't know how advertising works, why Potteresque fads and crazes occur, or what the marketing philosophy is, exactly. Mystery is a marketing tactic in itself. You have only to study the promotional practices of top-tier marketing organizations to appreciate that mystery, enigma, intrigue and "how do they do that?" are an important part of their matrioskha-doll–like appeal. Consider the "secret" recipes that help purvey all sorts of comestibles: Coca-Cola, Heinz Varieties, Kentucky Fried Chicken, Mrs Fields Cookies, Kellogg's Frosties, Grey Poupon Mustard, Brach's Chocolate Cherries, Angostura Bitters and, naturally, HP Sauce. Consider the gift-giving business, which is predicated on secrets, surprises and agonizingly delayed gratification, as are gift-rich occasions like Christmas, birthdays and St Valentine's Day. Consider the teaser campaigns, advertising soap operas and who'll-be-the-lucky-winner promotions that are launched daily by Machiavellian marketers. Consider the self-help marketing gurus who claim to possess the seven secrets of success, leadership, efficiency, effectiveness, time management, corporate well-being or, heaven help us, the Harry Potter Way to Higher Profits.

But how, I hear you ask, can we inject mystery into our organization, our product, our brand? Ah, that would be telling...

HELLO BOYS

A fourth lesson we can extract from the wonderful wizard of Hogwarts is, well, the importance of *wonder*. An ability to evoke consumer wonder is characteristic of extra-special brands. Great brands are wonder-full. They inspire. They intrigue. They surprise. They stimulate our senses. The look of an Alessi kettle. The feel of a Hermès scarf. The taste of Godiva chocolate truffles. The sound of an Aston Martin DB9. The smell of Chanel No. 5. Wonderful one and all.

According to Descartes, wonder is humankind's primal emotion.[2] It is our sense of wonder about the world we live in – why are things the way they are? – that has driven humanity from the dawn of time. Curiosity may have killed the cat, but it kitted us out with civilization, science and the (often wonderful) objects that surround us thanks to the wheelers, dealers, sellers and yellers of commercial life. A sense of wonder also delivered religion, spirituality and the belief systems that we turn to and live our lives by, consumerism included. True, the wonders of consumer society are as nothing compared to the natural wonder of rainbow-girt Niagara Falls, or Uluru at sunset, but in our desacralized and degraded world, wonderworking brands perform a similar function. Wonder is a numinous emotion. It is associated with the ineffable, the transcendent, the sublime. If, as someone once argued, the aim of marketing is to make the unbelievable believable, then marketing too is wonderful, wunderbar, merveilleuse.[3] Wonderbrands are what marketers should aim for and aspire to.

A HEARTBREAKING WORK OF MARKETING GENIUS

The dual meanings of wonder – curiosity and astonishment – come together in the fifth lesson, which pertains to the importance of storytelling. In chapter 1, and at various points throughout this essay, we noted that humankind is a storytelling animal. Philosophers, psychologists, anthropologists and theologists agree that for good or ill, we live our lives as narratives. Wonderbrands are storytellers too. Like wonderworking novels, they create fantasy places that consumers want to visit and project themselves into. Gucciworld, Nokialand, Virginville, Auditown, BlackBerry Way are mystical, magical, wonder-full settings that we desperately want access to. Products are the price of entry. We get telling tales in return.[4]

The Harry Potter brand tells us stories, sells us stories, and stories our selves for good measure. It isn't so much a great brand story as a great story brand. It generates a multitude of tales that act, interact, reinforce, contradict and occasionally undermine one another. It is a congeries of stories that bounce off each other like molecules in a cloud chamber or reflections in a hall of mirrors.[5] Harry Potter is the bouncing brand, the bouncy Hogwarts Castle of twenty-first-century marketing. Harry Potter reminds us that marketing is *fun*.

INVISIBLE HAND JIVE

Five lessons is enough for the meantime, I'm sure you agree, but I'll throw in one more for luck. And that concerns luck. Now, the concept of luck doesn't really exist in management science, much less in marketing research. Management commentators live in a nearly Newtonian universe. Everything is explicable, laws are inviolate, clockwork models obtain. The evidence, admittedly, suggests otherwise. History shows that happenstance plays a very big part in business. Procter & Gamble, perhaps the most "scientific" marketing organization ever, lucked out again and again and again. Harley-Davidson's latter-day triumph was four parts fluke to one part foresight. Arnold Schwarzenegger was hired to play the hero in *Terminator*, the good guy not the remorseless killing machine, and it was pure chance – a lunchtime chat with James Cameron – that tempted the C-list star of *Conan the Barbarian* to take on the role that made his career. Social scientists may not like it, but contingency, serendipity and accident are as important in business life as analysis, planning and control, possibly more so.[6]

On reading Rowling's own story, one can't help but be struck by the number of times the fates intervened. The series was a classic *coup de foudre*. It came to her complete, perfect, all of a sudden, out of the blue. She sent the MS to Christopher

Little's literary agency simply because she liked his name. Her slush-piled submission was read by an office worker at a loose end, and only because of its distinctive black plastic wallet. It landed on Bloomsbury's doorstep at the very moment when the publisher was developing its children's list. Scholastic picked Harry up at the urging of Janet Hogarth, who had previously worked for Bloomsbury, as luck would have it. Harry Potter wasn't David Heyman's first choice when he was looking for movie projects to develop, but his kids and a colleague persuaded him that the boy wizard was worth pursuing. Daniel Radcliffe was discovered by accident in a West End theatre, or so the publicity department informs us. And how can we forget Bloomsbury's marketeasing strategy, which it stumbled upon when the first print run was insufficient to meet demand and consumer desire expanded exponentially?

For all her undoubted storytelling skills, the bottom line is that Jo Rowling got lucky.[7] She won the literary lotto. She scooped the rollover of rollovers, the biggest jackpot there's ever been. As she herself observed in November 1997, "I am the luckiest person in the world." However, even in her wildest dreams she couldn't have imagined the luck that was still to come. Lady Luck looks after her own.

Magic matters.

The
Endnotes
Story

Chapter 1: The Introductory Story

1   In October 2004, *Forbes* calculated that the Harry Potter brand was worth $2.7 billion. However, this figure doesn't include the revenues from the Azkaban movie and its ancillaries (DVDs, CDs, computer games, etc.), which bring the total up to around $4 billion. Such estimates, incidentally, are pretty unreliable, though they are useful for marketing purposes, as I'll explain in chapter 4.

2   I first heard of Harry Potter in July 1999, when there was an item on the evening news about the phenomenon. Such was the excitement about the new Harry Potter book that schoolteachers feared children would skip class in order to buy it. However, rather than stand accused of inciting mass truancy, the great and good of Bloomsbury sagaciously decreed that *Harry Potter and the Prisoner of Azkaban* would go on sale at 3.45 p.m., when classes had finished for the day. As acts of corporate social responsibility go, this selfless bookselling decision hardly calls down the years. But you've got to admit it's a superb publicity stunt.

3   With the possible exception of those reliably obtuse High Court judges who remain ignorant of anything after *The Goon Show*.

4   Charles Leadbeater, *Living on Thin Air: The New Economy* (London: Viking, 1999).

5   The Chartered Institute of Marketing's ongoing campaign for hard-edged marketing typifies this fatuous quest.

6   On marketing magic generally, see my "Tore Down *à la* Rimbaud: Illuminating the Marketing Imaginary," in S. Brown *et al.* (eds), *Romancing the Market* (London: Routledge, 1998), pp. 27–54.

7   Alex Shakar, *The Savage Girl* (New York: Scribner, 2001).

8   For an excellent summary of all things narratological, check out H. Porter Abbott, T*he Cambridge Introduction to Narrative* (Cambridge: Cambridge University Press, 2002).

9   See, for instance, Stephen Denning, *The Springboard: How Storytelling Ignites Action in Knowledge-Era Organizations* (Oxford: Butterworth-Heinemann, 2000) and Stephen Denning, *Squirrel Inc.: A Fable of Leadership Through Storytelling* (San Francisco: Jossey-Bass, 2004).

10   Salman Rushdie, *Haroun and the Sea of Stories* (London: Granta, 1990).

Chapter 2: The Stories Story

1   The classic discussion of these issues is found in Northrop Frye, *Anatomy of Criticism: Four Essays* (Princeton, NJ: Princeton University Press, 1957).

2   J. K. Rowling, *Harry Potter and the Philosopher's Stone* (London: Bloomsbury, 1997).

3   J. K. Rowling, *Harry Potter and the Chamber of Secrets* (London: Bloomsbury, 1998).

4   J. K. Rowling, *Harry Potter and the Prisoner of Azkaban* (London: Bloomsbury, 1999).

5   J. K. Rowling, *Harry Potter and the Goblet of Fire* (London: Bloomsbury, 2000).

6   J. K. Rowling, *Harry Potter and the Order of the Phoenix* (London: Bloomsbury, 2003).

7   J. K. Rowling, *Harry Potter and the Half-Blood Prince* (London: Bloomsbury, forthcoming).

Chapter 3: The Author Story

1   She's already a dollar billionaire, according to *Forbes*. However, a recent investigation of Rowling's personal fortune by *The Scotsman* came up with the rather more conservative figure of £330 million.

2   Awarded to Jim Dale for his reading of *Goblet of Fire*. He was also nominated for his reading of *Sorcerer's Stone*.

3   If you need more detailed references for these facts and figures, dig up Stephen Brown, "Marketing for Muggles: The Harry Potter Way to Higher Profits," *Business Horizons*, 45 (1), 2002, pp. 6–14.

4   See, for example, Janet Brennan Croft, *War and the Works of J. R. R. Tolkien* (New York: Praeger, 2004).

5   The literary antecedents of "Hermione" are set out in Eliza T. Dresang, "Hermione Granger and the Heritage of Gender," in Lana A. Whited (ed.), *The Ivory Tower and Harry Potter* (Columbia: University of Missouri Press, 2002), pp. 211–42.

6 See Philip Nel, "You Say 'Jelly,' I Say 'Jell-O'? Harry Potter and the Transfiguration of Language," in Lana A. Whited (ed.), *The Ivory Tower and Harry Potter* (Columbia: University of Missouri Press, 2002), pp. 261–84.

7 Whatever you do, darling, don't mention the Cayman Islands tax shelter, much less the ass's milk on tap in the sunken bathroom.

8 Stephen Brown, "O Customer, Where Art Thou?," *Business Horizons*, 47 (4), 2004, pp. 61–70.

Chapter 4: The Books Story

1 Before you say anything, the proper translation of the tale is "The Princess on the Pea," not the more familiar "The Princess and the Pea." For a detailed discussion of the great storyteller's life and work, see Alison Prince, *Hans Christian Andersen: The Fan Dancer* (London: Allison & Busby, 1998).

2 This tale is recounted in countless Rowling biographies, for example, Sean Smith, *J. K. Rowling: A Biography* (London: Michael O'Mara Books, 2001).

3 On brand failures generally, check out Matt Haig, *Brand Failures: The Truth About the 100 Biggest Branding Mistakes of All Time* (London: Kogan Page, 2003).

4 John Hooper et al., "World Wide Wizard," *Guardian*, 8 November 2002, pp.14–15.

5 Colin Bateman, *Chapter and Verse* (London: Headline, 2003).

6 Jerry Palmer, *Potboilers* (London: Routledge, 1991).

7 Gabriel Zaid, *So Many Books: Reading and Publishing in an Age of Abundance* (Philadelphia: Paul Dry Books, 2003).

8 Articulate, rather.

9 Philip Nel tells the tale of Arthur Levine and his $105,000 bid for the US rights in *J. K. Rowling's Harry Potter Novels* (New York: Continuum, 2001).

10 The recommended retail price of *Phoenix* was £16.99. Tesco sold it for £9.97 in store (and £7.64 online), which was at or below cost, depending on who you talk to. Independent booksellers obviously thought so, because many purchased their stocks of *Phoenix* from Tesco! I think it's fair to assume that much blood will also be spilt over *Half-Blood Prince*. By the way, I'm not for a moment suggesting that the Harry Potter books lose money. Allow me some poetic licence here…

Chapter 5: The Cinema Story

1 It isn't called Rodeo Drive for nothing. And as for Pickett's Charge Card…

2 A full list of Rowling's favourite books is contained in Connie Ann Kirk, *J. K. Rowling: A Biography* (Westport, CT: Greenwood, 2003), appendix C.

3 The origin of this phrase, if memory serves, is H. Rider Haggard's classic boy's own tale, *She*.

4 Peter Kemp, *The Oxford Dictionary of Literary Quotations* (Oxford: OUP, 2003), p. 208.

5 Christopher Vogler, *The Writer's Journey* (Studio City, CA: Michael Wiese Productions, 1998).

6 Which is supplied in turn by Salman Rushdie's *Sea of Stories*. Presumably.

7 Ang Lee's *Hulk* and Tim Burton's *Planet of the Apes* leap to mind.

8 My statistical information source is the ever-reliable www.boxofficemojo.com.

9 The US and UK television rights, for example, were sold for $47 million and £10 million respectively. What's more, John Williams' soundtrack for *Sorcerer's/Philosopher's* topped the classical music charts in 2001.

10 It's not unusual for blockbuster movie sequels, such as *The Matrix Reloaded, Men in Black 2, Toy Story 2, Shrek 2* and *Return of the King*, to exceed the box-office takings of the originals. Harry Potter is a noteworthy exception to this rule. See Tom Shone, *Blockbuster: How Hollywood Learned to Stop Worrying and Love the Summer* (London: Simon & Schuster, 2004).

11 Stephen Brown, *Wizard! Harry Potter's Brand Magic* (London: Cyan, 2005), p. 78.

12 The genius of *Shrek 2* is that the main street of Never Never Land, Romeo Drive, features spoof fascias of Farbucks Coffee, Versachery, Baskin Robbinhood, Old Knavery, Gap Queen, Epiphany & Co., FeFiFo Schwarz and many more. So far so Hollywood. These parody brands, nevertheless, brilliantly echo the originals and *still* work as effective product placements. If anything, they are even more effective than standard product placements, since today's placements-savvy consumers are wise to cinematic tie-in shenanigans, and the parodies pander to this cine-literate constituency. They spoof and sell simultaneously.

Chapter 6: The Secrets Story

1 It's at www.jkrowling.com.

2 I discuss denial in detail in *Free Gift Inside!!* (Oxford: Capstone, 2003).

3 Tom Shone, *Blockbuster: How Hollywood Learned to Stop Worrying and Love the Summer* (London: Simon & Schuster, 2004), p. 26.

4 See *Free Gift Inside!!* (Oxford: Capstone, 2003), chapter 9.

5 John Maxwell Hamilton, *Casanova was a Book Lover* (Baton Rouge: Louisiana State University Press, 2000).

6 George Beahm, *Muggles and Magic: J. K. Rowling and the Harry Potter Phenomenon* (Charlottesville, VA: Hampton Roads, 2004).

7 *Free Gift Inside!!* (Oxford: Capstone, 2003).

8 Stephen Brown, "O Customer, Where Art Thou?," *Business Horizons*, 47 (4), 2004, pp. 61–70.

9 "The Fisherman and his Wife," in *The Complete Fairy Tales of the Brothers Grimm* (New York: Bantam Books, 2002), pp. 65–73.

Chapter 7: The Spin-offs Story

1 Ted Levitt, "Marketing Intangible Products and Product Intangibles," in *Levitt on Marketing* (Boston: Harvard Business School Press, 1992), pp. 75–83.

2 Tom Shone, *Blockbuster: How Hollywood Learned to Stop Worrying and Love the Summer,* (London: Simon & Schuster, 2004).

3   Jan Dalley, "It's a Kind of Magic," *Financial Times Magazine*,
17 May 2003, pp. 30–32.

4   Other examples include Allan and Elizabeth Kronzck's *The Sorcerer's Companion*, an A–Z primer on the real magic behind the fictional magic of the series; Gary Wiener's *Readings on J. K. Rowling*, an anthology of critical writings on the author, including the infamous demolition jobs by Harold Bloom and William Safire; and Guy Macdonald's *The Harry Potter Quiz Book*, no fewer than 1001 questions, at three levels of difficulty, on the boy wizard's imperishable corpus. Several anthologies of press clippings, children's letters, author interviews and plot-line speculations have also been published.

5   Kennilworthy Whisp, *Quidditch Through the Ages* (London: Whizz Hard Books, 2001); Newt Scamander, *Fantastic Beasts and Where to Find Them* (London: Obscurus, 2001).

6   Clarke, in particular, has benefited from Bloomsbury's Harry-honed marketing muscle. *Jonathan Strange & Mr Norrell* was longlisted for the 2004 Man Booker Prize and garnered rave reviews in the United States. Hollywood is already knock, knock, knocking on Susanna's door.

7   When the publication date of *Half-Blood Prince* was announced on 21 December 2004, Bloomsbury's share price surged 7 percent to a new all-time high of £2.94. The book immediately soared to number 1 on Amazon's bestseller list, a full seven months before publication.

8   This issue is described in detail by Philip Nel in *J. K. Rowling's Harry Potter Novels* (New York: Continuum, 2001).

9   Incidentally, only 30 percent could spell Shakespeare correctly. Mind you, as the Swan of Avon couldn't spell his own name correctly, today's mis-spellers can hardly be condemned outright.

10   FYI, I found this nugget in Emma Jones' excellent *Literary Companion* (London: Think Publishing, 2004).

Chapter 8: The Critics Story

1   Nor is this retelling an attempt to settle the score. How could you think such a thing, gentle reader?

2 Anthony Holden, "Why Harry Potter Doesn't Cast a Spell Over Me," *Observer Review*, 25 June 2000, pp. 1–2.

3 Harold Bloom, "Can 35 Million Book Buyers Be Wrong? Yes," *Wall Street Journal*, 11 July 2000, p. A26.

4 Jack Zipes, "The Phenomenon of Harry Potter, or Why All the Talk?," in *Sticks and Stones: The Troublesome Success of Children's Literature from Slovenly Peter to Harry Potter* (New York: Routledge, 2001), pp. 170–89.

5 A. S. Byatt, "Harry Potter and the Childish Adult," *New York Times*, 7 July 2003; www.nytimes.com.

6 In France, for instance, Potter provoked a spat between leading public intellectuals, one arguing in *Le Monde* that Harry was a capitalist apparatchik, another contending that he's a right-thinking, left-leaning, anti-capitalist class warrior at heart. In Germany, meanwhile, the cerebral classes worry about the untold psychological damage the boy wizard is doing to future generations, filling their heads with charms, spells and all sorts of dangerous hocus pocus.

7 See Philip Nel, *J. K. Rowling's Harry Potter Novels* (New York: Continuum, 2001).

8 Harold Bloom, "Can 35 Million Book Buyers Be Wrong? Yes," *Wall Street Journal*, 11 July 2000, p. A26.

9 See www.eulenfeder.de/hpliteratur.html.

10 Eliza T. Dresang, "Hermione Granger and the Heritage of Gender," in Lana A. Whited (ed.), *The Ivory Tower and Harry Potter* (Columbia: University of Missouri Press, 2002), pp. 211–42.

11 See www.sfxbrown.com.

12 For detailed discussion of the religious objections to HP, see Richard Abanes, *Harry Potter and the Bible: The Menace Behind the Magick* (Camp Hill, PA: Horizon Books, 2001).

13 Quoted in Emma Jones, *Literary Companion* (London: Think Publishing, 2004).

14 Felicity Kendal, "Harry Potter is a Triumph, but a Classic? I Don't Think So," *Daily Telegraph*, 19 July 2003; www.opinion.telegraph.co.uk.

15 John Harlow and Maurice Chittenden, "Movie Pirates Cash In on Harry Potter Mania," *Sunday Times*, 4 November 2001, p. 24.

16 "Harry Potter and the Merchandising Gold," *The Economist*, 21 June 2003, p. 78.

17 Stephen Brown, *Marketing – The Retro Revolution* (London: Sage, 2001).

18 This is the post-industrial equivalent of J. K. Galbraith's Countervailing Power precept. It's a kind of Countervailing Culture.

Chapter 9: The Consumers Story

1 Walter Benjamin, "The Storyteller," in *Illuminations* (London: Fontana, 1973), p. 83.

2 Quoted in Robert McKee, *Story* (London: Methuen, 1997), p. 11.

3 Known as slash fiction, this particular strand of the "fanon" puts the perv into Impervious, the dung into Mundungus, the butt into Butterbeer, the arse into Parselmouth, the homo into Alohomora, the rim into Grim, the wood into Oliver, as it were, and does things with Engorgement Charms that you don't want to know about. Believe me.

4 Pravina Patel, "Harry Potter Fans Start Boycott of Film Merchandise," *Mail on Sunday*, 25 February 2001, p. 35.

5 A useful overview of the fan community literature is found in Matt Hills, *Fan Cultures* (London: Routledge, 2002).

6 Rick Gekoski, *Tolkien's Gown* (London: Constable, 2004), p. 223. Re W. B. Yeats's marketing prowess, see my "Chronicles of the Celtic Marketing Circle, Part I," *Marketing Intelligence and Planning*, 18 (6/7), 2000, pp. 400–13.

7 Rebecca Sutherland Borah, "Apprentice Wizards Welcome: Fan Communities and the Culture of Harry Potter," in Lana A. Whited (ed.), *The Ivory Tower and Harry Potter* (Columbia: University of Missouri Press, 2002), pp. 343–64.

8 Suman Gupta, *Re-reading Harry Potter* (Basingstoke: Palgrave, 2003).

9 You may wonder why I'm studying young adults rather than children.

Harry Potter's peers – that is, the kids who were 11 in 1997, the year the first book was published – are now at university. They have left HP behind demographically. I'm trying to discover if they're leaving him behind permanently.

10 For further reflections on Harry Potter's future – plus the secret of the series' denouement! – take a gander at the free downloadable chapters on my website, www.sfxbrown.com.

Chapter 10: The Brands Story

1 See Douglas B. Holt, *How Brands Become Icons* (Boston: Harvard Business School Press, 2004).

2 Matt Haig, *Brand Royalty* (London: Kogan Page, 2004).

3 Stephen Brown, *Postmodern Marketing* (London: Routledge, 1995).

4 Leslie de Chernatony, *From Brand Vision to Brand Evaluation* (Oxford: Butterworth-Heinemann, 2001).

5 Marina Warner, *Signs & Wonders* (London: Vintage, 2003), p. 392.

6 Wally Olins, *On Brand* (London: Thames & Hudson, 2003), p. 18.

7 Raymond L. Lee and Alistair B. Fraser, *Rainbow Bridge: Rainbows in Art, Myth and Science* (University Park, PA: Pennsylvania State University Press, 2001). Incidentally, I'm not suggesting that rainbow brands don't exist. They do. But the rainbow metaphor has never been exploited by the consultancy industry as far as I'm aware.

8 Christopher Booker, *The Seven Basic Plots: Why We Tell Stories* (London: Continuum, 2004).

Chapter 11: The Concluding Story

1 I jest, m'lud.

2 Philip Fisher, *Wonder, The Rainbow and the Aesthetics of Rare Experiences* (Cambridge, MA: Harvard University Press, 1998).

3 Yes friends, I was that soldier. *See Marketing – The Retro Revolution* (London: Sage, 2001).

4 I discuss this further in Stephen Brown and John F. Sherry, Jr (eds), *Time, Space and the Market: Retroscapes Rising* (Armonk, NY: M. E. Sharpe, 2003).

5 Corporate storytelling, let's be frank, faces exactly the same fate as that predicted for Harry Potter. The fad will implode. The bubble will burst. The end is nigh. Harry Potter isn't simply a role model for teenagers of all ages. He's a model for brand consultants, market researchers and those who ply their proprietary wares to managerial markets. Harry Potter can teach everyone lessons, even those who teach lessons for a living. *Especially* those who teach lessons for a living.

6 The ultimate irony is that physical scientists openly acknowledge that we live in a world of uncertainty, indeterminacy and discontinuity. Whether it be the chance mutations of evolutionary theory, the baffling postulates of quantum theory or the non-linear systems of chaos and complexity theory, unpredictability is the watchword of our inexplicable times, except among B-school blind watchmakers.

7 On the subject of luck, see Jackson Lears, *Something for Nothing* (New York: Viking, 2003) and Gerda Reith, *The Age of Chance* (London: Routledge, 1999).

DATE DUE